What T]
About *Heads Bowed*

Lisa Mladinich brilliantly combines the Church's *Lectionary*, feast days, and liturgical seasons with the prayer tradition of dedicating the days and months to specific devotions. *Heads Bowed* is at once spiritual, liturgical, and doctrinal—an ideal aid for beginning your instruction, or your day, in prayer and union with God. It belongs in every Catholic parish, classroom, and home.

> —**Marc Cardaronella**, director, Bishop Helmsing Institute for Faith Formation, Diocese of Kansas City-St. Joseph and former parish director of religious education

Heads Bowed is your go-to prayer resource for instilling the gift of daily prayer in the hearts and souls of children. Chock-full of beautiful, inspirational meditations, this book is perfectly designed to lead you and your children into daily conversation with God. I expect my copy will be dog-eared from daily use. I can't wait to pray with this beautiful book!

> —**Lisa M. Hendey**, founder of CatholicMom.com and author of the *Chime Travelers* series

Many Catholics have shared with me that they don't know how to pray. The Our Father and the Hail Mary, yes. But what's missing for them is a way to enter more deeply into dialogue with Christ, his mother, the saints, and our Church community. *Heads Bowed* helps adults and children in their care to pray meaningfully together during the school year, whether at school or at home. With prayers for each day of class, this book is a wonderful companion for our spiritual walk. To that, I say, "Amen!"

> —**Elizabeth Ficocelli**, speaker, radio host, and author of *Seven From Heaven: How Your Family Can Find Healing, Strength and Protection in the Sacraments*

One of the greatest gifts we can give our students is a love of prayer. Lisa Mladinich gives educators and students alike a wonderful gift in this book that inspires a new generation of believers to appreciate the richness of our Catholic faith. From the Holy Trinity to the communion of saints to the rosary and even to virtues like unity, gratitude, reverence, and mercy, a wide variety of topics and vocabulary are reinforced in these prayers and help teach children what they can offer to God.

—**Jared Dees**, creator of TheReligionTeacher.com, author of *To Heal, Proclaim, and Teach*

This prayer book is perfect for Catholic students and teachers, but I admit to wanting a copy for my home, too! It's full of inspiration and practical wisdom and sure to be an invaluable resource for all who use it.

—**Sarah Reinhard**, author, blogger at SnoringScholar.com

Not just for Catholic school teachers, this wellspring of inspiration will be used regularly in our homeschool. Lisa Mladinich inspires through a deep, personal connection with both student and subject and teaches by loving. You will love this book.

—**Karen Edmisten**, author of *You Can Share the Faith: Reaching Out One Person at a Time*

Heads Bowed

Prayers for
Catholic School Days

Lisa Mladinich

Liguori

Imprimi Potest:
Stephen T. Rehrauer, CSsR, Provincial
Denver Province, the Redemptorists

Published by Liguori Publications
Liguori, Missouri 63057

To order, visit Liguori.org or call 800-325-9521.

Library of Congress Cataloging-in-Publication Data

Names: Mladinich, Lisa, author.
Title: Heads bowed : prayers for Catholic school days / Lisa Mladinich.
Description: First Edition. | Liguori : Liguori Publications, 2017.
Identifiers: LCCN 2016021984 (print) | LCCN 2016023680 (ebook) | ISBN
    9780764826443 (paperback) | ISBN 9780764870767 (ebook)
Subjects: LCSH: Catholic children—Prayers and devotions. | Catholic
    teachers—Prayers and devotions.
Classification: LCC BX2198 .M53 2017 (print) | LCC BX2198 (ebook) | DDC
    242/.82—dc23
LC record available at https://lccn.loc.gov/2016021984

Liguori Publications, a nonprofit corporation, is an apostolate of the Redemptorists. To learn more about the Redemptorists, visit Redemptorists.com.

Printed in the United States of America
21 20 19 18 17 / 5 4 3 2 1
First Edition

Contents

INTRODUCTION

Teaching by Loving

"For me, prayer is a surge of the heart; it is a simple look turned toward heaven, it is a cry of recognition and of love, embracing both trial and joy."

—Thérèse of Lisieux,
quoted in the *Catechism of the Catholic Church*, 2558

Leading children of various temperaments and backgrounds to a life of prayer is a long and challenging task. Prayer is that uniquely individual opportunity to be awestruck by the Father, to gaze adoringly at Jesus, to be docile to the Holy Spirit. But without the firm and grace-filled foundation formed by prayer, it is impossible to do anything else of worth. So we must begin by trusting that God completes what we leave unfinished and blesses our small efforts.

Few things are more compelling than a good example. To sense the tender devotion of a beloved adult is a powerful beacon of love that attracts the budding spiritual consciousness of a little boy or girl to a natural contemplation of their own mysterious relationship with God. Like a toddler in a spring garden reaching out to touch the brightly colored blossoms, a young soul can be attracted by the joyful beauty of reverence, the peacefulness of a life of faith, the efficacy of prayerful petition, and the delicate aroma of sanctity. To teach a child to pray requires that the teacher or parent be a person of prayer, too.

One of my favorite series in literature is *Anne of Green Gables*, in part because of the character Anne Shirley's profound and poetic appreciation for beauty and the delightfully funny and very human growth we observe in her life of faith. But she is also a gifted and passionate teacher, and her methods are authentically Christian. Rather than ruling her little schoolhouse with an adversary's fearful authoritarianism, hers is a method that inspires through a deep, personal connection with both pupil and subject. In her own quirky imitation of Christ, she teaches by loving. While fictional, she is believably effective.

In the last few years, I have often contemplated the reality that God actually dwells within me. Many of the saints have prayed without ceasing by practicing an awareness of God's presence in the quiet of their souls. I am sometimes filled with awe, putting my hand over my heart and praying these words: "You are here within me. I love you. I praise you." Prayer can be that spontaneous and brilliantly simple.

Yet, we have at our fingertips a myriad of beautiful and powerful prayer traditions through our beloved Catholic Church, and they are also important to our understanding of the winsome mysteries of our faith. Each of us is linked together in the body of Christ through our sacramental lives, sacred Scripture, feast days, and the liturgical seasons of Advent, Christmas, Lent, Easter, and Ordinary Time. In fact, through longstanding tradition, each day is dedicated to a specific devotion:

Monday: The Holy Spirit and the Souls in Purgatory
Tuesday: The Holy Angels
Wednesday: St. Joseph
Thursday: The Blessed Sacrament
Friday: Christ's Passion and His Sacred Heart
Saturday: The Blessed Virgin and Her Immaculate Heart
Sunday: The Resurrection and the Holy Trinity

Even our months are dedicated:
January: The Holy Name and Childhood of Jesus
February: The Holy Family
March: St. Joseph
April: The Blessed Sacrament
May: Mary
June: Sacred Heart of Jesus
July: The Precious Blood
August: Immaculate Heart of Mary
September: Seven Dolours (Sorrows) of Mary
October: The Holy Rosary, the Holy Angels,
   and Respect for Life
November: Holy Souls in Purgatory
December: The Immaculate Conception

Since each jewel in our liturgical year presents a clue to the heavenly treasures we seek—day by day, week by week, and month by month—they help us to reflect with fresh insight on the great love God has for us. With the aid of sacred Scripture, the holy and living word of God, we are able to discover a more immediate sense of God's individual call to every human heart.

It is also of great importance to note the efficacy of the holy rosary (October's dedication), a devotion of great power. Many converts, myself included, were drawn to Christ through the recitation of the rosary, and countless holy men and women have entrusted their spiritual, moral, and physical safety to the Blessed Mother's beautiful chaplet of love.

Sr. Lucia dos Santos, one of the seers at Fatima, explained the power of the rosary this way:

"The Most Holy Virgin in these last times in which we live has given a new efficacy to the recitation of the Rosary to such an extent that there is no problem, no matter how difficult it is, whether temporal or above all spiritual, in the personal life of each one of us, of our families...that cannot be solved by the Rosary. There is no problem, I tell you, no matter how difficult it is, that we cannot resolve by the prayer of the Holy Rosary."

Many saints and venerable spiritual figures in the history of the Catholic Church have encouraged a love for this powerful prayer, which is a tender contemplation of the mysteries of our redemption found in the Gospels and dogmas of Holy Mother Church. A decade of the rosary only takes about five minutes, so consider adding at least that much to your daily routine with the children. We would all be greatly blessed by meditating on the twenty mysteries represented by Mary's little circle of beads, each one calling us closer to the spirit of the Gospels and to the hearts of Jesus and Mary. How rich we are! Let's enjoy and share these treasured mysteries with our children, a little at a time.

Joyful: The Annunciation to Mary, the Visitation of Mary and Elizabeth, the Nativity of Our Lord, the Presentation in the Temple, the Finding of the Child Jesus in the Temple

Sorrowful: The Agony in the Garden, the Scourging at the Pillar, the Crowning With Thorns, the Carrying of the Cross, the Crucifixion of Jesus

Glorious: The Resurrection, the Ascension of Our Lord, the Descent of the Holy Spirit on the Apostles, the Assumption of the Blessed Virgin Mary into Heaven, the Coronation of Mary as Queen of Heaven

Luminous: The Baptism of the Lord, the Miracle at Cana, the Proclamation of the Kingdom and the Call to Repentance, the Transfiguration of Our Lord, the Institution of the holy Eucharist

I hope this book of prayers will help you invite the children in your care into the prayerful life of the Church; into an intimate, trusting, and personal relationship with Jesus Christ; and into the great communion of saints, preparing the way of the Lord, and journeying to their ultimate home with God, in heaven.

The first two chapters offer prayers for parents, catechists, and teachers as they prepare for the start of the school year. Prayers for forty-eight weeks are for use with the children. The actual school year is normally about thirty-six weeks long (180 days, not counting holidays), but the start and end dates of school districts, parishes, and homeschools can vary tremendously. Therefore, extra weeks have been offered to allow greater flexibility and continuity. Every chapter begins with a Bible verse, providing a rich theme for the prayers of that week, while the prayer for each of the five days represents a unique catechetical opportunity, with both spiritual and practical applications of the Scripture for everyday life. Vocabulary words are noted in some chapters; a glossary at the end of the book defines them.

Feel free to use this collection as it is presented, according to the weeks of the school calendar, or use the weeks or days in whatever ways suit you and the children in your care. At the end of the weekday prayer sections, you will find a selection of thirty-four prayers for special occasions. I pray these, too, will help you to enjoy the school year in a spirit of prayer and trust in Almighty God.

You are doing something wonderful for the children and for yourself. Count on my prayers for a glorious and fruitful year. God bless you!

Special note: *While the first two weeks of prayers are designed to support you as you prepare for the start of the school year, the themes are useful any time you need a spiritual boost or a moment of private prayer. Feel free to return to these early pages often.*

SECTION ONE

Prepare the Way of the Lord

Week 1:
Strength in Weakness

As you prepare to start the school year, can you make time for extra prayer? Humbling yourself to pray for God's assistance opens the floodgates of his grace.

...He said to me, "My grace is sufficient for you, for power is made perfect in weakness." I will rather boast most gladly of my weaknesses, in order that the power of Christ may dwell with me. Therefore, I am content with weaknesses, insults, hardships, persecutions, and constraints, for the sake of Christ; for when I am weak, then I am strong.

2 Corinthians 12:9–10

Day 1: Come, Holy Spirit. Bless me as I prepare to receive into my heart the children God has ordained for me to teach this year. Bless the children and their families as they wind down their summer vacations and once again start to turn their hearts toward academic learning. I ask that the holy souls in purgatory watch over the children and pray for them without ceasing until they, too, enter heaven. I offer the future merits of all our work and prayers to alleviate the sufferings of the holy souls, that they might sooner enter the beatific glory of heaven and the joy of their eternal salvation. Amen.

Day 2: Holy angels, you surround us with your prayerful and protective presence at all times, and I thank you. I ask that you watch over our classroom throughout the coming year, filling it with your praises to God and guarding it diligently with your holy presence and your powerful prayers. Draw down from heaven every grace and blessing we need to heal our wounds, repent of our sins, and offer our sufferings in union with the cross of Jesus Christ for the good of souls. Amen.

Day 3: Humble St. Joseph, chaste spouse of the Blessed Virgin Mary, you protected and nurtured the Holy Family. Now I ask for your prayers and your protection for everyone who will work and learn in this school/parish/home. As I set up my classroom, prepare my materials, and plan for the school year, intercede for me, that I might give over every anxiety to God, trust in his holy will, and rejoice humbly in the role that I am called to play in the lives of the precious children entrusted to me. Saint Joseph, you who received guidance through angelic messages in dreams, please grant that, as I ponder the coming school year, I will sense God's guiding presence in my soul and trust completely in his merciful love for me and for the children. Amen.

Day 4: Into your shining presence, dear Lord, I come in a spirit of humility and trust. Help me to believe that as I cultivate virtue in my own life—one moment, one hour, and one day at a time—the interior radiance of my soul will increase along with my trust in you. Offer me the grace that empowers me to bear witness to your saving love. Open all of our hearts to your holy word as you speak through every prayer and every lesson. Bless us and give us a hunger for holiness that will make this school year a time of deep joy and increasing hope. Amen.

Day 5: Jesus, holy Lamb of God, my precious Lord, help me to embrace the sacrificial love of the cross as I tend to the countless details of preparing for the coming school year. It is hard for me to face them all, and sometimes I am anxious that time will run out before I can complete everything. Help me to trust that because you created time and live outside of it, you also bless time as part of your creation and that you bless my use of time. Remind me each time I look at my watch or consult the clock that you entered into time as a helpless baby to be with us and to journey with us in our humanity. Thank you, Jesus. Amen.

Day 6: Mary, conceived without original sin, you are my mother and the Mother of the Church. Please mother and console me as I prepare to lead and inspire the children entrusted to my care. Mother them, too, and bring them every grace and blessing that will help them find their holy purpose in God's plan, as we learn together, day by day. Blessed Mary, ever Virgin, pray for us. Amen.

Day 7: Most holy and undivided Trinity, I praise you for your glory and for the holy sacrifice of the altar. In your unlimited generosity, in the gift of Jesus' precious body and precious blood, you offer me eternal salvation, though I can never deserve it. In humility, I offer to you, in this holy Eucharist, every moment of the coming school year: every lesson, every conversation, every joy, every sorrow. While ordinary failures are sure to come through our flawed humanity, the triumphs of grace will be your gift to our efforts. I ask with confidence that you bless all my efforts—past, present, and future—that they bear holy and beautiful fruit in my life, in the lives of my students, and in the lives of all our loved ones. I praise you in advance for these gifts of grace. Amen.

Week 2:
Empowered by Christ

Do you feel overwhelmed by the work ahead of you?
Give every anxiety to Jesus and he will bless you with greater faith
and a more certain sense of your God-given authority.

Then Jesus approached and said to them, "All power in heaven and on earth has been given to me. Go, therefore, and make disciples of all nations, baptizing them in the name of the Father, and of the Son, and of the holy Spirit, teaching them to observe all that I have commanded you. And behold, I am with you always, until the end of the age."

Matthew 28:18–19

Day 1: Holy Spirit, you fill the universe with your gentle light, give me a keen intuition to know what each child needs to thrive spiritually, socially, and intellectually. Help me remember with compassion that each child has both gifts and limitations ordained by God through age, temperament, and personality, and that I am a temporary caretaker of these precious souls, beloved by God. Amen.

Day 2: Angel guardian, you hold me in your hand, even as you behold the face of God in heaven. Bless all my teaching materials and lessons as I pull them together for the coming year. Allow me to use them with great love and with humble confidence in your intercessory powers. Help me to remember that any time I am in the presence of other human beings, I am also in the presence of their guardian angels. How awesome is the love of God, who surrounds us with such love, beauty, power, and protection. Amen.

Day 3: St. Joseph, under your pious title, "Glory of home life," I ask for your prayers in all that I do for the children, whether in my home, my parish, or my school. Where children feel loved and accepted, pardoned and encouraged, they feel at home. Teach me patience and humility so that every child has a chance to flourish as Jesus did in your tender care. Saint Joseph, pray for us. Amen.

Day 4: Jesus, bread of angels, feed my soul. Fill it to overflowing with love of you so that every life I touch will be touched by your love. Heal me of anything that keeps me from loving you whole-heartedly. Enable me to serve you in freedom each day and with ever-increasing devotion and joy. Let that joy pour out into my work and relationships, drawing others to embrace you in the sacrament of the Eucharist. Amen.

Day 5: Jesus, your heart is called the "abyss of all virtues." Draw me into this holy abyss and saturate my soul with a love of virtue and every grace needed to bring that love to fruition. Teach me to be prudent, just, courageous, temperate, chaste, generous, humble, and diligent. Strengthen me with the theological virtues of faith, hope, and love—your gifts to those who ask. Amen.

Day 6: Blessed Mother, help me to appreciate every child entrusted to my care and to rely on your help at all times. Each human person is made in the image and likeness of God. Help me to see the face of Christ in every child every day, no matter how challenging our interactions might sometimes be. If a child is being exceptionally difficult, remind me to pray for him, that his hidden crosses be made lighter and his heart be comforted. When I need wisdom, I trust you to provide it. Mary, seat of wisdom, pray for me and help the children have a great first day of school. Amen.

Day 7: Holy God, undivided Trinity, bless our learning community with a spirit of cooperation and love. God the Father, God the Son, and God the Holy Spirit, you are a loving and joyful family of the highest magnitude. Inspire me and the children I will teach this year, with a desire to serve each other with generous hearts. Make my teaching vibrant and impactful, and make my efforts to communicate with parents and caregivers clear and effective so that they hear the love and concern in my words and become cooperators in my humble efforts. Amen.

Day 8 (the night before classes start): Tomorrow is the big day, Lord. Thank you for helping me get ready. I place all the children and every moment of the coming school year into your loving hands. Fill me with confidence in a strong beginning to our school year, and help me to persevere in faith through each quarter, drawing power from your holy love and the prayers of the saints and holy souls. I offer you all my efforts in advance for every intention that lives in my heart, especially the salvation of souls. I dedicate and consecrate this school year to Jesus, through Mary. Amen.

SECTION TWO

Welcoming
the Children

Week 3:
Blessings for a New School Year

Did you know that when you work hard and love everyone,
you become more and more like God?

Vocabulary: wisdom, Eucharist, divine

And this is my prayer; that your love may increase ever
more and more in knowledge and every kind of perception,
to discern what is of value, so that you may be pure and
blameless for the day of Christ, filled with the fruit of right-
eousness that comes through Jesus Christ for the glory and
praise of God.

Philippians 1:9–11

Day 1: Holy Spirit, when we come to you in prayer, your great power strengthens our hearts and minds with **wisdom** and love. We know that praying together is powerful, and we offer you all our love and the joy of this new school year. Give us joy in learning and love for one another. Help us to be grateful for the gift of our education, since many children in the world are not so fortunate. We ask you to bless and protect the poor children of the world, and we ask the holy souls in purgatory to pray for them and for us every single day. Thank you, Lord, for bringing us all together. Amen.

Day 2: Lord, you have given each of us a guardian angel, and we are so happy to have this powerful, heavenly friend at our side throughout our lives. Our guardian angel prays for us until the very moment we enter heaven. We can always turn to this spiritual friend for help with schoolwork, with friendships, and with any problems. Thank you, God, for giving us such a powerful and holy companion. Amen.

Day 3: Dear, humble St. Joseph, you raised the Child Jesus with great love and patience. You taught him to be a carpenter and protected him from harm. You are like a father to us, too. You watch over the whole Catholic Church and cover us in your powerful prayers. As we pray and learn together, please help us to be more like you: to have pure thoughts, generous hearts, and deep trust in the powerful love of God. Thank you for your example of patience, courage, and love. Amen.

Day 4: Jesus in the holy **Eucharist**, adored by countless angels, you are present to us at **Mass** in four ways: through the host at Communion, through the priest who stands at the altar, through the words of the Bible, and in all of us gathered together in your name. We are all members of the body of Christ, the Church. Remind us each day that we are carriers of your **divine** love and that we should always try to see your face in every other human face—no matter who we are with and what is happening in our lives. Amen.

Day 5: Dear Jesus, your heart is full of goodness and love. Your death on the cross showed us that pain offered out of love for others can change the world. Help us treat each other with kindness. If we are in a bad mood, help us offer that suffering for those who may have disappointed us or hurt us. We love you. We adore you. And we ask you to fill our hearts with your divine love so that we may share that love with others every day. Amen.

Week 4:
True Happiness

Can you tell about a time when
doing something hard brought you joy?

Vocabulary: diligent, rituals, soul, intercession, purpose, sacred

> *Now, children, listen to me; happy are they who keep my ways. Listen to instruction and grow wise, do not reject it! Happy the one who listens to me, attending daily at my gates, keeping watch at my doorposts; For whoever finds me finds life, and wins favor from the LORD.*
>
> Proverbs 8:32–35

Day 1: Come Holy Spirit, and help us to be **diligent** in our studies and our chores. When Jesus was a child, he had to work hard to learn the Scriptures as well as the prayers and **rituals** of his faith. He even worked side by side with his foster father, St. Joseph, and became a skilled carpenter. Because he loved and honored those who taught him, he learned his lessons well and was able to help others. By doing our very best, we become more like Jesus and discover two secrets to happiness: hard work and a generous spirit. Amen.

Day 2: Heavenly Father, you are the source of all love, light, and joy. Because I am your child, you will never abandon me. You have placed a guardian angel by my side to watch over me and pray for my **soul**. Help me to remember this holy but invisible friend and to invite my celestial guardian to come with me everywhere I go. Give me wisdom through my angel's holy **intercession** so that every day of my life, all my prayers and actions will move me closer to God, step by step. Amen.

Day 3: Dear St. Joseph, your life was filled with beauty and **purpose** because you served God with trust in his will, no matter what. Sometimes God's will was spoken to you by angels who appeared to you in dreams. Each time the angels appeared, you obeyed right away, even if the angel's message seemed strange to you. Pray for us and for all students around the world so that God's holy and beautiful purpose for our lives will become clearer each day. Amen.

Day 4: Jesus, through the holy Eucharist, you give us all that is good, true, and beautiful. You are the answer to every question and every problem. You are the source of all that makes us truly happy. Help us to treat others so kindly that they will know we are Christians. Give us the courage to speak about you to anyone who may not know you. Help us to forgive those who hurt us, as you forgave those who betrayed and wounded you, even when you were suffering on the cross. Jesus, we thank you for loving us and sharing your life with us. Amen.

Day 5: Mary, you are our mother most amiable, and you love each of us more than we can imagine. Today is Friday, which is dedicated to the **Sacred** Heart of your dear Son, Jesus. Please help us to honor Jesus through our love for others as we look for many small ways to cheer each other up and help in any way we can. Sometimes just giving another person a smile or a kind word is enough to turn a stressful day into a happy, creative one. We know that Saturday is your special day, Blessed Mother, so please help us to honor you by finding ways to be generous and kind this weekend, too. Amen.

Week 5:
Respect for Authority

*Why is it important to obey our teachers, parents,
and other loving adults?*

Vocabulary: eternal, inspire, authority, blessing, gift, grace, sacrifice, infinite, fail

> *Obey your leaders and defer to them, for they keep watch over you and will have to give an account, that they may fulfill their task with joy and not with sorrow....May the God of peace, who brought up from the dead the great shepherd of the sheep by the blood of the **eternal** covenant, Jesus our Lord, furnish you with all that is good, that you may do his will. May he carry out in you what is pleasing to him through Jesus Christ, to whom be glory forever. Amen.*

> Hebrews 13:17, 20–21

Day 1: Come, Holy Spirit. **Inspire** us to work hard this week and to treat our pastors, teachers, parents, and other adults with respect. We know that proper **authority** always comes from God, so when we obey we actually do something holy. When we learn to respect the rules of our homes, parishes, and schools, we learn something priceless: we learn to respect ourselves. Help us to be humble and ready to obey, Lord, so that we never miss a chance to grow in wisdom. When we respect your authority, we respect ourselves. Amen.

Day 2: Holy guardian angels, you are all around us. We salute and honor you because you are obedient to God at all times.

Thank you for your holy prayers for us. Because you are faithful, we can trust in your powerful protection, as you guide us safely home to heaven, step by step and day by day. Shine the light of understanding into our hearts to help us do God's will in the present moment. Amen.

Day 3: Dear Lord, you provide for all our needs out of the kindness of your heart. Thank you for this day and for our family, friends, food, clothes, books, and every other **blessing** in our lives. We know that the very best **gift**s you give us are invisible, hidden in our souls. Because we are baptized, our souls are ready to receive your **grace**, which is a share in your own life, love, and power. Lord, let us never forget how blessed we are to be your children. Fill our hearts with the joy of our salvation, and help us share it with each other. Amen.

Day 4: Jesus, you feed us with your precious Body and Blood at holy Communion. Even if we are too young to receive you in the Eucharist, we know that you are truly present at Mass and that you hear our prayers and feed our souls with grace. We thank you for this gift of yourself. Help us to give our time and talents freely, to be ready to listen, and to work cheerfully for the good of others. Since you are present to us, we will try our best to be present to each other. Amen.

Day 5: Sacred Heart of Jesus, you **sacrifice**d your own precious life to save us from darkness and sorrow. You love us so much every moment. Not even the worst sin could make you stop loving us. We trust in your **infinite** mercy to heal us and make us whole, no matter how many times we **fail** to be honest, patient, or generous. Help us to appreciate the sacraments of holy Eucharist and reconciliation, two precious and powerful gifts that heal our souls, bring us joy, and prepare us to live with you for all eternity in heaven. Amen.

Week 6:
Imitating Jesus

How would you describe Jesus in just a few words?

_____

Vocabulary: yoke, burden, begotten

> *Take my **yoke** upon you and learn from me, for I am meek and humble of heart; and you will find rest for yourselves. For my yoke is easy, and my **burden** light.*

Matthew 11:28–30

Day 1: Lord Jesus, you have shown us how to live by giving us the example of your own life. We read in the Bible that, never asking anything for yourself, you taught others about the Father's love; you healed and blessed the people who came to you in pain and sorrow; you fed them with food blessed by your own hands; and when they were sorry for their sins, you forgave them and restored their joy. We don't know how to find that joy on our own, but when we do our best to turn away from sin and follow you, we fill up with a holy love that flows out to all those around us. Thank you for showing us your ways. Amen.

Day 2: Heavenly Father, your only **begotten** Son, Jesus, humbled himself to become human like us. He didn't swoop down in a golden chariot or arrive with the sound of war drums and a huge, supernatural army. He was born into poverty and lived a life of humble service, and then he offered his own life to pay for our sins. When he was suffering without complaint on the cross, he was thinking of how much he loved us and wanted to save our souls. Lord, help us all to think less of ourselves and more about the needs of others so that we can follow in your way of peace. Amen.

Day 3: Blessed Mother and St. Joseph, your family life with Jesus was filled with tenderness, compassion, and joy. With the help of your prayers, we hope to imitate the love that you shared and make our families and classrooms safe and welcoming places for everyone to learn and grow. Teach us to open our hearts to each other and give generously of our time and concern. Holy Family, pray for us. Amen.

Day 4: My Jesus, sometimes we are afraid to imitate you. We think that if we try to be good and avoid doing anything wrong we will seem strange to other people. But when we live in a way that pleases you, we are kinder and more joyful. Our friendships are stronger and our lives are filled with meaning. So what are we afraid of? The world needs your love, and we are called to share that love. There is nothing more important. Thank you for giving yourself to us in the sacraments, especially holy Eucharist. Amen.

Day 5: Sacred Heart of Jesus, you have showed us by your death and resurrection that all of our sufferings can have power, too, because they can be gifts of love. When we experience loneliness, worry, sickness, fear, or sadness and offer it to you as a gift, you turn that pain into power and save souls. You can turn any problem in our lives into something beautiful. We thank you and we praise you, Lord Jesus. Amen.

SECTION THREE

Respect for All
God's Children

Week 7:
The Holy Rosary

*What are some ways we can be more pleasing
to our Blessed Mother, Mary?*

Vocabulary: adore, Blessed Sacrament

Standing by the cross of Jesus were his mother and his mother's sister, Mary the wife of Clopas, and Mary of Magdala. When Jesus saw his mother and the disciple there whom he loved, he said to his mother, "Woman, behold, your son." Then he said to the disciple, "Behold, your mother." And from that hour the disciple took her into his home.

John 19:25–27

Day 1: Blessed Mary Ever Virgin, we offer this new school week to Jesus through your all-powerful intercession. Thank you for praying for us in every moment of our lives. You are our sweet, gentle mother, and your prayers protect us from danger and help us to grow closer to Jesus. Remind us to love your holy rosary, the most powerful prayer there is, after the holy Mass. Help us to appreciate the gift of our lives and learn to love generously, like Jesus. We love you, Blessed Mother. Amen.

Day 2: Heavenly Father, children's prayers are very powerful, which is why the angel of peace appeared in glory to the shepherd children at Fatima and taught them a special prayer. The angel told them not to be afraid and to always believe, **adore**, love, and hope in Jesus in the **Blessed Sacrament**. The angel also taught them to pray every day for those who do not yet believe or have hope in Jesus. Lord, make us fearless Christians, and use our prayers to save other children, born and unborn. Amen.

Day 3: Our Lady of Fatima, just as you instructed the shepherd children at Fatima to pray the rosary every day, we should pray the rosary, too. By learning the Apostles' Creed, the Our Father, the Hail Mary, the Glory Be, and the Hail Holy Queen, we walk with you and with your divine Son, Jesus, in a powerful way. Inspire us, dear Mother, to learn our prayers by heart, so we can easily pray at least one decade of the rosary every day. Thank you for being our mother. Amen.

Day 4: Our Lady, the rosary is a powerful weapon that protects us from danger and helps us avoid sin. You have promised that those who pray the rosary every day will be your special children and receive many powerful gifts from heaven. The rosary helps us to grow in our appreciation of the gifts of faith, like wisdom, virtue, joy, and peace, and even life itself. Your holy love lights our path, refreshes our souls, and draws us closer to Jesus. Mother most pure, help us to be prayer warriors, strengthened by the most holy rosary to save souls for Jesus. Amen.

Day 5: My Jesus, your heart was pierced on the cross. When that happened, our Lady's heart was pierced, too. She is the most wonderful mother who has ever been or ever will be. She suffered greatly out of compassion for you. Because you chose to become human, even though you remained fully divine, you became a brother to each and every one of us, and your mother became our mother, too. Help us to love her as much as you do. Thank you, Jesus. Amen.

Week 8:
The Path of Life

How does God protect you when you're afraid?

_____

Vocabulary: exhort, dwell, secure, Sheol, the pit, mercy

> *I bless the LORD who counsels me; even at night my heart*
> ***exhort**s me. I keep the LORD always before me; with him at*
> *my right hand, I shall never be shaken. Therefore my heart*
> *is glad, my soul rejoices; my body also **dwell**s **secure**, for*
> *you will not abandon my soul to **Sheol**, nor let your devout*
> *one see **the pit**. You will show me the path to life, abound-*
> *ing joy in your presence, the delights at your right hand for-*
> *ever.*

Psalm 16:7–11

Day 1: Most Holy Trinity—Father, Son, and Holy Spirit—my life is precious to you, even when I feel like I'm all alone. You never leave my side and you have a beautiful plan for my life. Even though I sometimes wonder if you've forgotten me, down deep I know you are very close. On my worst days, you are there to help carry my crosses. Help me to count my blessings so that I will always have a joyful heart. My God, I trust in you. Amen.

Day 2: Heavenly Father, thank you for guiding my life in so many ways. You've given me your holy word in the Bible, the Ten Commandments that help me live my best life, and loving adults who guide me and teach me. Your love pours into my life like the waters of my baptism, bringing me joy and hope. Help me to spread that joy and hope to everyone I meet today. Amen.

Day 3: Jesus, you are the way, the truth, and the life. Following in your way of love and **mercy** is the only way to happiness. When I see someone who is sad or lonely, or if I see someone not being nice, help me remember that you are hidden in their hearts. Give me the courage to use words of peace and friendship. Thank you for your friendship, Jesus. Amen.

Day 4: Lord, you are all that is good and holy. You know that sometimes it is difficult for me to do the right thing. I am often tempted to do what I want or what someone else wants instead of what you want me to do. But you are always at my side, so I know that I'm never alone, even when I am afraid. Help me to have faith that you are always with me and that your love for me is very powerful. Like St. Paul, I know that when I am weak I am strong because I am leaning on your strength. Amen.

Day 5: Dearest Jesus, every life is created through your Sacred Heart. We are made out of your love. Every person belongs to you and when I treat them well, you are very happy with me. Help me to love all people, even when it is very hard. I know that your love can bring great joy to challenging situations, so when I have a hard time being nice to someone, I will say a silent prayer and offer my efforts to help save souls. Some day in heaven, I will meet the souls saved through my prayers and offerings. I love you, Jesus. Amen.

Week 9:
The Unborn

Is it ever hard for you to speak up about what is right?

Vocabulary: glorious, temple

> *The word of the LORD came to me: Before I formed you in the womb I knew you, before you were born I dedicated you, a prophet to the nations I appointed you. "Ah, Lord GOD!" I said, "I do not know how to speak. I am too young!" But the LORD answered me, Do not say, "I am too young." To whomever I send you, you shall go; whatever I command you, you shall speak. Do not be afraid of them, for I am with you to deliver you.*

Jeremiah 1:4–8

Day 1: **Glorious** God, you have known me and loved me since before you created me. My life is part of your plan to save the world. Every person is a treasure to you, and every baptized person is a **temple** of the Holy Spirit. Help me to respect myself by saying my prayers every day, eating good food, going to bed on time, and exercising daily. Most of all, help me to love you and follow you in all that I say and do. Today I offer my prayers and work for the holy souls in purgatory. Amen.

Day 2: Dear Jesus, St. Anselm taught that, from the moment we are created in our mother's womb, God gives us a guardian angel to watch over us. We are precious to God no matter how small we are. Even though we are hidden away for a little while before we are born, God always sees us and loves us. After we are born, God's angel stays with us throughout our lives and guides us safely to God when we die. Our angel will not leave us or stop praying for us until we are ready to enter into the joy of heaven. Amen.

Day 3: Dear St. Joseph, before Jesus was born, an angel told you to watch over Mary and Baby Jesus, and you did. You took amazing care of the little Son of God and Mary, even though you had to work very hard as a carpenter to feed your family. Thank you for praying for our families. Ask God to give us the courage and strength to protect all unborn babies and to love our own families as much as you love Jesus and Mary. Amen.

Day 4: Dear Jesus, at holy Communion many of us receive your precious Body and Blood, and this holy food helps us grow strong in faith, hope, and love. Just being in your presence at Mass strengthens us. Even though we are young, your presence makes us powerful prayer warriors. Help us to remember to pray every day. Thank you, Jesus, for giving yourself to us, body and soul. Amen.

Day 5: Jesus, we are all members of your family and members of your body, the Church. When we treat each other kindly, we treat you kindly. If we are not kind to others, we are not kind to you. But our sins don't change the fact that every life is holy and loved by God. Thank you, Jesus, for loving us, no matter what. Help us to treat everyone the way we would treat you. Amen.

Week 10:
Speaking Respectfully

Why does God tell us to use only words that are kind and true?

Vocabulary: foul, grieve, mock, confession, radiant, trust-worthy, meek

> *Therefore, putting away falsehood, speak the truth, each one to his neighbor, for we are members one of another... No **foul** language should come out of your mouths, but only such as is good for needed edification, that it may impart grace to those who hear. And do not **grieve** the holy Spirit of God, with which you were sealed for the day of redemption. All bitterness, fury, anger, shouting, and reviling must be removed from you, along with all malice. [And] be kind to one another, compassionate, forgiving one another as God has forgiven you in Christ.*
>
> Ephesians 4:25, 29–32

Day 1: Lord Jesus, when you were being **mock**ed and beaten by the Roman soldiers, you did not show anger. You were gentle and calm. You are all-powerful and could have ordered an army of angels to come and protect you, but you accepted suffering to save us from our sins. When I use unkind words or treat another person in a mean way, I sin, and that makes you sad. Please help me remember that every person is a child of God. I should never use words or actions that hurt, even if it seems funny to me. Give me the courage to say, "I'm sorry" when I do something wrong and to get to **confession** as soon as I can. Amen.

Day 2: Lord, like the angels, we are called to be messengers of love to all we meet. Teach us self-control in choosing the words we use to speak with one another. Remind us that it is in serving others that we meet you and become more like you. Kind words can be an act of service. Help us to build each other up and to make it easier for others to believe that Christ is present through our words and actions. Jesus, you are alive in my heart. Help me to shine with your **radiant** love. Amen.

Day 3: Lord, you are the God of all that is good, beautiful, and true. It offends you when I tell a lie or fail to tell the whole truth. Help me to be careful to always speak the truth so that I will grow up to be a **trustworthy** person. I know that you can always see into my heart, and you know when I am trying to be good, even though I make mistakes. I can never hide from you, and I wouldn't want to. Thank you for never growing tired of forgiving me. Amen.

Day 4: Jesus, sometimes your name is used in a way that is unkind, as if it were a bad word. We know you are the kindest person who has ever lived and that your name is holy and beautiful. Your name, Lord Jesus, should be said with love. Just saying "Jesus" can be a powerful prayer. Jesus, my Jesus, I love you. Today I offer all my good works and prayers in honor of your holy name. Amen.

Day 5: Jesus, you are the glorious Son of God and our almighty Savior. And yet you were **meek** and humble when others were cruel to you. Your heart is so kind that you would never yell at us or use foul language, even if we did something very sinful. Help us remember that we are strong and courageous when we are kind, and that mean or ugly words make us weak. Thank you for your mercy, Lord. Amen.

Week 11:
The Benefits of Kindness

How can we make up with people after we hurt their feelings?

Vocabulary: deeds, repent, confess

Kindly people benefit themselves, but the merciless harm themselves. The wicked make empty profits, but those who sow justice have a sure reward. Justice leads toward life, but pursuit of evil, toward death. The crooked in heart are an abomination to the LORD, but those who walk blamelessly are his delight.

Proverbs 11:17–20

Day 1: Most Holy Trinity, the good things we do make us stronger, while the bad things we do make us weaker. Give us the desire to be saints so we can be our best, happiest selves. It is an amazing fact that our baptism gives us enough grace to become saints. You are generous. Help us to trust in your grace every day and never give up on becoming holy. Help us to love you in the Eucharist, in the holy words of the Bible, and in every person we meet. Amen.

Day 2: Lord, it is amazing that you allow each of us to be a part of your divine plan. When we offer you our prayers, homework and chores, good **deeds**, joys, and even our sadness, you are happy with our gifts and pour out graces on the world. Our small offerings become like money in your heavenly bank. Hidden acts of love, like cleaning up a mess we didn't make or silently doing someone else's chore are very powerful offerings to you. Thank you for letting us help save souls. Amen.

Day 3: Dear Jesus, we know that the good we do is very powerful when we give it to you as a gift, but you are even more wonderful than that. Even the times we have done something bad on purpose can be offered to you as soon as we are sorry. It makes you very happy when we **repent**, and it brings us joy when we run to you for forgiveness. Being truly sorry means that we do whatever we can to make things right again, say we're sorry to the person we hurt, go to confession, and work hard to do better in the future. Thank you for your mercy, Lord. Amen.

Day 4: Lord Jesus, when we **confess** our sins to the priest at church, we know that you are really and truly there with us. It is you who forgives our sins. Every time we confess, you give us more and more grace. The graces of confession help heal our souls and make us stronger. If we have not made our first confession at church, we can always pray to you in private and ask our parents for help in doing better. Some day, we will have the joy of the sacrament of reconciliation. Thank you, Jesus. Amen.

Day 5: Sacred Heart of Jesus, when we are loving, generous, forgiving, and joyful, we are like you. Help us even when we're sad, to have a spark of your joyful love in our hearts. Help us to see the needs of others all around us. Is someone in our home, neighborhood, or school feeling sad, angry, or lonely? Would it help if I listened to that person's problems and tried to be a friend? Does someone need help with a hard task or a kind word of encouragement? Give us the grace and the courage to be aware of others and ready to help. Thank you for the way you are always a friend to us. Amen.

SECTION FOUR

The Communion
of Saints

Week 12:
The Holy Souls

Can you name a loved one who has already died?
Would you like to pray with the class for his or her soul?

_____

Vocabulary: archangel, console, mystery

*We do not want you to be unaware, brothers, about those who have fallen asleep, so that you may not grieve like the rest, who have no hope. For if we believe that Jesus died and rose, so too will God, through Jesus, bring with him those who have fallen asleep...For the Lord himself, with a word of command, with the voice of an **archangel** and with the trumpet of God, will come down from heaven, and the dead in Christ will rise first. Then we who are alive, who are left, will be caught up together with them in the clouds to meet the Lord in the air. Thus we shall always be with the Lord. Therefore, **console** one another with these words.*

1 Thessalonians 4:13–14, 16–18

Day 1: Most Holy Trinity, you are three divine persons in one divine nature, a perfect and beautiful family overflowing with infinite love. The Catholic Church is part of your family, too. That includes all of the baptized people here on earth, the souls in purgatory, and the saints and angels in heaven. Thank you, Father, Son, and Holy Spirit, for making us your adopted children and welcoming us into this amazing family. We praise you for your love and your goodness, and for the joy we look forward to: living with you forever in heaven. Amen.

Day 2: Angel of God, my guardian and friend, sometimes I'm sad because people I know have been very sick or hurt. Some of them have even died. Pray for me to have a strong faith and believe with all my heart that everyone who trusts in God and tries to be good will live together forever in heaven some day. Help me to believe in the resurrection of Jesus Christ and the glory of God the Father. Thank you, my angelic friend, for helping me to have faith. Amen.

Day 3: God, you love us so much that you sent your Son, Jesus, to teach us, to heal us, and to die for our sins. When we have faith in you, our hearts fill up with the light of your love and we find happiness. Jesus said, "I am the resurrection and the life; whoever believes in me, even if he dies, will live" (John 11:25). Help us, Lord, to believe in Jesus and follow him all the way to heaven. Amen.

Day 4: Dear Jesus, some day in heaven we will get to hear your voice. When we look at the Eucharist, we know that you are really there, but you are hidden and silent. It is a great **mystery**. The Bible tells us that some day your voice will call out to us. When you return to earth to gather us all together we will hear glorious sounds of archangels and trumpets coming from heaven. We praise you and bless you, we glorify you. Come, Lord Jesus. Amen.

Day 5: Sacred Heart of Jesus, sometimes we need you to wrap us up in your love and help us feel peaceful again. Life can be very hard, especially when someone we love dies. When your friend Lazarus died, you cried, even though you knew you were going to raise him from the dead. You showed us that it's OK to cry, even though we believe we will be together again in heaven some day. Thank you for understanding how we feel and walking with us in our grief. Amen.

Week 13:
Saints and Angels

What sin will you ask your guardian angel to help you overcome?
Think about this in silence.

Vocabulary: endure, crucifixion

> *Therefore, since we are surrounded by so great a cloud of witnesses, let us rid ourselves of every burden and sin that clings to us and persevere in running the race that lies before us while keeping our eyes fixed on Jesus, the leader and perfecter of faith. For the sake of the joy that lay before him he **endure**d the cross, despising its shame, and has taken his seat at the right of the throne of God.*

Hebrews 12:1–2

Day 1: Lord, we are surrounded by heavenly friends: angels, archangels, saints, and the holy souls in purgatory. They watch us and cheer for us, praying for us as we do battle with our sins. They are so happy when we ask them for their prayers, and they love to pray for us. Help us to remember that the holy souls in purgatory need our prayers to help them enter into heaven. Thank you for giving us such an amazing family. Amen.

Day 2: Dear Lord, the Bible tells us that each of us has an angel at our side, a powerful spirit who loves us and prays for us all the time. Let's greet the angels that are here with us, now. Holy angels, please work together to help us all to be friends and to treat each other with great love, in Jesus' name. Amen.

Day 3: Dear Jesus, you call us to be heroes, like you. You were willing to suffer and die for us because you knew that the gift of your life would open the gates of heaven for us. Help us to remember that when we suffer, we should always have hope, because you can make good things come from anything bad. We praise you for being with us in the hard times, and we thank you for the graces that pour into our lives when we trust you. Amen.

Day 4: God, you are pure and perfect, but I can never be pure and perfect without your help. I want to turn away from sin and be holy like you. I know it pleases you when I try my best to be good. In fact, it pleases you when I just want to be good, even when I fail. Give me the grace to keep trying because you love me no matter how many times I fall into sin. Your grace is enough for me. I praise you, my Lord and my God. Amen.

Day 5: Sacred Heart of Jesus, you sit on your throne, glorious and perfect, in heaven, at the right hand of God the Father. Yet, you still have the wounds of the **crucifixion** on your hands and feet and side. We know that by your wounds we are healed (see Isaiah 53:5). Help us to remember that our fears, hurts, and sadness are wounds, too. Each wound is an open door, leading us to your love. Thank you for being with us in our suffering. Amen.

Week 14:
Thanksgiving

What is the most beautiful part of God's creation, to you? People?
Animals? The stars and planets? The sky? The ocean?
The beauty of growing things? The rain? Something else?

Vocabulary: awe, universe

For everything created by God is good, and nothing is to
be rejected when received with thanksgiving, for it is made
holy by the invocation of God in prayer.

1 Timothy 4:4–5

Day 1: Most Holy Trinity, you created all things: the glorious stars and planets, mountains, trees, oceans, animals, wind, snow, and rain. All of creation and all people come from your heart and belong to you. Fill us with joy and **awe** at how amazing your **universe** really is, and inspire us to be good stewards of all you have given us. We praise you for your beautiful world. Amen.

Day 2: Dear Jesus, we are so thankful for all the gifts we receive each day. We know that when we say grace before meals, you really do bless us and our food. Help us to never waste healthy foods, and—even if we don't like the taste—help us to be grateful that we have enough to eat, especially when so many children in the world are hungry. Thank you for being so generous with us, Lord. With your help, we want to be generous, too. Amen.

Day 3: Lord, the Ten Commandments are more than just rules. Everything you give us is a beautiful gift. Behind every "no" in the Ten Commandments is a much bigger "yes." Telling us not to lie means that you love the truth and that we are happier when we are truthful. Telling us not to steal means we should be generous and helpful if we want to find our greatest joy. You only want what is best for us. Thank you for showing us how to be holy and happy. Amen.

Day 4: Jesus, you told your apostles that where two or more people pray together, their prayers are very powerful. The same is true for us. When we are all together like this, talking with you, you are right here with us. You listen to us and are happy to be with us. Give us the grace to believe that you hear all of our prayers and answer them, even if we have to be patient waiting for your answer or don't get the answer we want. We love you, Lord. Amen.

Day 5: Lord, we ask you to bless us as we look forward to the weekend. Bless our busy times and quiet times, our times of work and times of play. Help us to remember to pray every day and to participate with love in the holy Mass on Sunday. If we can't get to Mass for some reason, please come to us in our hearts. Amen.

Week 15:
Love of the Church

Did you know that you are all members of the body of Christ?
The Church would not be complete without you.

Vocabulary: pledge

Let the word of Christ dwell in you richly, as in all wisdom you teach and admonish one another, singing psalms, hymns, and spiritual songs with gratitude in your hearts to God. And whatever you do, in word or in deed, do everything in the name of the Lord Jesus, giving thanks to God the Father through him.

Colossians 3:16–17

Day 1: Heavenly Father, the Bible is full of amazing stories about your love for us. It tells us how you made the whole universe out of nothing and how you helped your people to be holy. Thank you for so many exciting stories of faith, like the shepherd boy David facing the giant, or the great judge, Judith, who defeated a whole army all on her own. The Bible tells us how you sent us your Son, Jesus, to save us from our sins. Help us to love our Bibles. Amen.

Day 2: Lord, you are always ready to give us beautiful gifts of grace. You are so generous and kind. We are all part of one holy family, and we should help each other to be good. Please give us the gift of wisdom so we will be able to tell right from wrong, and give us the gift of courage to speak up when we see someone doing anything that is hurtful or dangerous. Thank you, Lord, for helping us to be better friends to each other. Amen.

Day 3: God, you love it when we sing songs of praise and thanksgiving. It helps us to be happy when we count our blessings and sing about how good and kind you are. When we practice being thankful, you bless us with joy. When we think about you and sing to you, we grow closer to you and become more like you. Thank you for lifting our hearts to you, Lord. Amen.

Day 4: Dear Jesus, you have given us everything because you have given your whole self on the cross and in the holy Eucharist. Everything good and holy is found in you, because you are God and you are all good and all holy. You are the answer to every problem, every question, every prayer we can ever think up. We offer our whole day to you in honor of your many gifts to us. Thank you for the gift of yourself. Amen.

Day 5: Sacred Heart of Jesus, in your holy name we offer you this day and the coming weekend. We give you our schoolwork, our friendships, the food we enjoy, the games we play, and every song and prayer. In your name, we **pledge** our best efforts to be kind to everyone. Bless us, Lord, and make us holy by your free gifts of grace and mercy. Amen.

SECTION FIVE

Advent and Christmas

Week 16:
God in the Ordinary

Did you know that God shows his glory
in ordinary people, places, and events?
Can you name one way God shows his glory in your life?

_____

Vocabulary: prophet

> *But you, Bethlehem-Ephrathah least among the clans of Judah, From you shall come forth for me one who is to be ruler in Israel; Whose origin is from of old, from ancient times.*
>
> Micah 5:1

Day 1: Lord, sometimes I feel so small. I feel like I'll never do anything very important. I wonder, how can such an amazing God pay attention to an ordinary kid like me? But you tell us in the Bible that you have a plan for each child, even before we are born (see Jeremiah 1:5). You love every single one of us very much. Your powerful love gives me hope that if I give my life to you each day, you will make each day amazing. I love you, God. Amen.

Day 2: God, sometimes our lives are very noisy and we miss out on the beauty of your presence. Long ago, when you spoke to the **prophet** Elijah, he heard your voice in a gentle breeze—not in the earthquake, the hurricane, or the forest fire. Please help me prepare my heart to receive Jesus by speaking gently to everyone I meet. Help me to notice the quiet and shy people around me. Thank you for your gentle ways. Amen.

Day 3: Dear St. Joseph, because of your obedience to the holy angels, God's amazing plan was able to happen. You loved Jesus and Mary and kept them safe. When Jesus grew up, he changed the world with his teachings, his healings, his mercy, and his sacrifice. Help us to remember that when ordinary people do their best to follow God, he uses them to do great things. Humble St. Joseph, pray for us. Amen.

Day 4: Jesus, present in the Blessed Sacrament, you are so good and so kind. You are ready to help us any time we ask. When we look at the host, we only see a round piece of bread. It looks so ordinary and plain. And yet you are really with us in the Eucharist, and we can ask your help with any problem or tell you about our hopes and dreams. Thank you for coming to us on earth in the holy Mass. Amen.

Day 5: Dear Jesus, your heart is humble and pure. When you walked the earth, you knew that some people would hate you for speaking the truth about God and about sin, but you kept doing what was right anyway. Help us to remember that what people think of us doesn't matter. It is enough to try our best to be good and kind, like you. Please remind us that when we fail to be kind, you are there with your mercy to help us make it right again. Give us the grace to trust in you so we can become holy like you. Amen.

Week 17:
Others Before Myself

What can you do today to practice loving others more than yourself?

If there is any encouragement in Christ, any solace in love, any participation in the Spirit, any compassion and mercy, complete my joy by being of the same mind, with the same love, united in heart, thinking one thing. Do nothing out of selfishness or out of vainglory; rather, humbly regard others as more important than yourselves, each looking out not for his own interests, but [also] everyone for those of others.

Philippians 2:1–4

Day 1: Lord, you love it when we act like a family, with our hearts full of love for each other. Help us cheer each other on and help each other succeed. To be a true family—whether in a classroom, our parish, or in our home—means thinking of others more than we think of ourselves. When I help others, I discover the joy of being close to you, my God. Thank you for helping me to be my best self. Amen.

Day 2: Dear guardian angels who guard each person in this room, sometimes we can get annoyed with the people around us. We need your help to stay peaceful and to work together out of love for God. Each of the angels in this room right now is special, powerful, and beautiful in its own way, and every angel lives for God alone. Holy angels, pray for us so we will become holy like you. Amen.

Day 3: St. Joseph, patron of the Catholic Church, you are an amazing saint. We know that you protected Jesus and Mary and worked very hard without complaining. Pray for us so we may be humble, cheerful, and hard-working like you. If we start each day with prayer and try our best to do everything for Jesus, the way you did, our lives will fill up with joy. Thank you for praying for our souls every day. Amen.

Day 4: Jesus, when we were baptized, our souls were changed forever. The Holy Spirit washed us clean and made us into temples of God's love. Help us to remember that you live within us, Lord, and that every time we are kind to another person, we are kind to you. Help us to love you with all our hearts, Jesus, so we will love and forgive everyone. Amen.

Day 5: Dear Jesus, sometimes when I make a bad mistake, I get very sad. Help me remember that your heart is so sweet that you love forgiving my sins. You know how hard it can be for me to make good choices, and when I am sorry for my sins, I make you happy again. Your mercy is amazing. Help me to show mercy to others by finding something good in every person I meet. I want to share your gentle love with the world. Amen.

Week 18:
Love for Parents and Caregivers

*What are some ways we can show respect and honor
to our parents and caregivers today?*

Vocabulary: beloved

*Children, obey your parents [in the Lord], for this is right.
"Honor your father and mother." This is the first command-
ment with a promise, "that it may go well with you and that
you may have a long life on earth."*

Ephesians 6:1–3

Day 1: Lord God, you are a Father to us in the best possible ways. You love us, you protect us, and you provide for us. You bless us with people on earth who care about us, teach us, and help us to be our best selves. Inspire us to keep our hearts and minds open to those who are such a gift to our lives. Help us listen and obey every godly command, knowing that you bless us for saying yes to those who help us do your will. We love you, heavenly Father. Amen.

Day 2: Holy Mother Mary, when Jesus was dying on the cross, he told St. John to love you as his own mother. Jesus also told you to love John as your own son. We are your children, too, and we are so happy that you love us and pray for us every day. Be our queen and rule our hearts so we can grow up in the joy of your friendship. We want to be just like you: holy and obedient to God. We love you, Mary. Amen.

Day 3: Holy St. Joseph, Mary was created without any sin in her heart, and Jesus could never sin. Yet Jesus obeyed you, because you were his **beloved** foster father. Jesus knew that the Bible commanded him to obey and respect his parents, but he also knew that you were happy to be obedient to God the Father. Help us learn to be holy through obedience. Amen.

Day 4: Jesus, you obeyed your heavenly Father when he asked you to come to earth to save us from our sins. God the Father was very pleased with your "yes" and opened the gates of heaven to us. You showed us that when we obey God, he makes our lives powerful and beautiful. Thank you, Jesus. Amen.

Day 5: Sacred Heart of Jesus, your heart is so kind and generous that we want to obey your laws and give glory to your holy name. You have made a beautiful world for us to live in. You make the sun rise in the morning and you bring out the moon and stars at night. You make the flowers grow up toward the light, just as you call us to reach our hearts up toward your shining love. Thank you for making our lives so rich. Amen.

Week 19:
Gifts of Love

What gifts can you give to others this Christmas?
Think about what you can do for them or make for them with love.

Vocabulary: bountifully, compulsion, wretched, tabernacle

Consider this: whoever sows sparingly will also reap spar-
*ingly, and whoever sows **bountifully** will also reap bounti-*
fully. Each must do as already determined, without sadness
*or **compulsion**, for God loves a cheerful giver. Moreover,*
God is able to make every grace abundant for you, so that
in all things, always having all you need, you may have an
abundance for every good work. As it is written: "He scat-
ters abroad, he gives to the poor; his righteousness endures
forever." The one who supplies seed to the sower and bread
for food will supply and multiply your seed and increase the
harvest of your righteousness.

2 Corinthians 9:6–10

Day 1: Dear God, you shower your gifts of love on us as we prepare to celebrate the birth of Jesus. It is such an exciting time
of year. Help us remember every single day that it is more important to give than to receive, and that we should do all our
work with a smile. You love it when we are generous like you, so
please give us the grace to be helpful and cheerful out of love for
you. Amen.

Day 2: Heavenly angels, pray that our hearts will be full of love for Jesus and inspire us to smile at everyone we meet. The joy of our love for God is powerful and helps show other people the way to heaven. When we choose to smile instead of complaining or being impatient, we reveal one of the secrets of true happiness and peace on earth: courage. Amen.

Day 3: St. Joseph, solace of the **wretched**, remind us that when we are very happy and excited, there is always someone in the world—sometimes a person close by—who is suffering. Help us to offer all of our joys, sorrows, work, and celebration for souls so that God will rain down blessings from heaven on all who ask for his help. We know that God blesses every good that we do and multiplies it like seeds that bring a bountiful harvest. Amen.

Day 4: Sweet Jesus, your birthday was the day you gave all of yourself to save us—body and soul. Help us to prepare for your birthday by giving of ourselves to others, too. When we offer to do extra work at home or to help someone in our neighborhood or school, we brighten their day and show them your love, Jesus. Lamb of God, help us to be like you and make your birthday even happier. Amen.

Day 5: Dear Jesus, send your Holy Spirit to fill us up with joy whenever we are at Mass, because you are there waiting for us in the **tabernacle**. If we try our best to pay attention and celebrate the holy Mass reverently, we know that you will bless us and give us your joy. That joy will be a gift to others and spread like wildfire. Help us to remember that the Eucharist is really you, and that receiving you is the greatest gift of all. Amen.

Week 20:
Christmas

What will you do to make someone else happy today?

_____

Vocabulary: hymns

> *For God so loved the world that he gave his only Son, so that everyone who believes in him might not perish but might have eternal life. For God did not send his Son into the world to condemn the world, but that the world might be saved through him.*

> John 3:16–17

Day 1: Holy Spirit, you brought Jesus to earth through your divine power. Thank you for giving us the best Christmas gift of all. Our Lord Jesus is a gift beyond price. Inspire us, O Lord, to love the Baby Jesus and carry him in our hearts at all times. When we fail, give us the grace to return to Jesus and confess our sins, since he always loves us, no matter what. Praise be to God the Father, the Son, and the Holy Spirit. Amen.

Day 2: Glorious angels, you announced the birth of Jesus to the poor shepherds, and you surround us with **hymns** of praise to God, right here and now. Some day in heaven we will be able to hear your beautiful songs of joy and celebration, and we will join you in singing them. Holy and glorious angels, pray for us to have joyful hearts. Amen.

Day 3: St. Joseph, you watched over Mary and Jesus and kept them safe in Bethlehem and on the long roads you traveled together afterward. Because you loved them both so much and took such good care of your Holy Family, our Savior was able to grow up strong and healthy and save the world from sin. Remind us that our lives have a purpose, too, and that taking good care of each other is a part of God's plan to save the world. Amen.

Day 4: God, when I think about Jesus coming to earth, I realize that he must love each of us very much. Jesus is God and can do anything he wants to, but he chose to become a helpless baby born to poor parents, to teach us that love is what makes us rich. Remind us that when his mother laid him in a manger that animals eat out of, Jesus was already teaching the world that he would one day become our spiritual food. Amen.

Day 5: Most Sacred Heart of Jesus, when you were born on Christmas, you became the sacrament of divine love, showing us how to live a holy life. When you come to us in the Blessed Sacrament at Mass, you humble yourself once again, hiding within the simple appearance of bread and wine. Receiving you into our hearts and bodies brings holiness to our souls. Thank you, Jesus. Be reborn in our hearts every day. Amen.

Week 21:
Gratitude

Did you know that it pleases God when we sing songs of joy to him? What Christmas hymn should we sing?

_____

Vocabulary: wondrous, resound, exult

> *Give thanks to the LORD, invoke his name; make known among the peoples his deeds. Sing praise, play music; proclaim all his **wondrous** deeds....Let the heavens be glad and the earth rejoice; let them say among the nations: The LORD is king. Let the sea and what fills it **resound**; let the plains be joyful and all that is in them! Then let all the trees of the forest **exult** before the LORD, who comes, who comes to rule the earth...Let all the people say, Amen! Hallelujah!*
>
> 1 Chronicles 16:8–9, 31–33, 36

Day 1: God, our hearts are still shining with Christmas joy. There is no gift more precious or more exciting than the gift of your divine Son, Jesus. Help us to make Baby Jesus happy by being thankful for every blessing, whether we received it under the Christmas tree or through the kind words and actions of the people who care about us. Help us to be grateful for all the ways we sense your gentle presence among us. Amen.

Day 2: Heavenly angels, help us to praise God the way you do: for the gift of our homes, our schools, and the gift of our parish church, where we learn about all that is good and holy. Help us to be grateful for the work we are given and to give it our full attention, especially the subjects that are hardest for us. Guardian angels, thank you for helping us understand and appreciate our lessons. Amen.

Day 3: Lord, you have blessed us in many ways that we are not even aware of. Help us to see your love in the beauty of the natural world around us and in all the ways we are able to do wonderful things. Especially help us to see your love in all the ways that we are weak and afraid, because they show us how much our true strength comes from you. We praise you, God. Amen.

Day 4: Jesus, as members of your Church, we are members of your precious body. You are the Prince of Peace, and we are your royal people who love you and honor you with our lives. Even when we do something wrong, you are quick to forgive us. When we are sorry for our sins, you love us even more. Your love fills up the whole earth, the seas, the skies, and the universe. We praise you, Lord Jesus, for making us one family in your love. Amen.

Day 5: Merciful God, thank you for another school week full of fascinating ideas, facts, and experiences that help us appreciate the amazing world you have created for us. Just struggling to learn strengthens our minds and souls. We know that you bless our efforts and make good come from them. Help us to remember that when we help others learn, we help them draw closer to God, the source of all knowledge. Amen.

Week 22:
Mary, Mother of Jesus

What do you love most about the Blessed Mother?

_____

Vocabulary: mantle, reverent

A great sign appeared in the sky, a woman clothed with the sun, with the moon under her feet, and on her head a crown of twelve stars. She was with child.

Revelation 12:1–2

Blessed are you, daughter, by the Most High God, above all the women on earth; and blessed be the Lord God, the creator of heaven and earth, who guided your blow at the head of the leader of our enemies. Your deed of hope will never be forgotten by those who recall the might of God. May God make this redound to your everlasting honor, rewarding you with blessings, because you risked your life when our people were being oppressed, and you averted our disaster, walking in the straight path before our God.

Judith 13:18–20

Day 1: Dear Mary, because of your pure and courageous heart, you became the mother of the whole Church—our heavenly mother. Whenever we are afraid, worried, or sad, please wrap us in your blue **mantle** of peace and protection, and shower us with graces from heaven. Teach us how to trust God no matter what is going on around us. Hail Mary, full of grace, the Lord is with thee. Amen.

Day 2: Holy Mary, our Catholic Church calls you the "Mother of God" because you are the mother of Jesus, God's divine Son and our king. In ancient times in Israel, the mother of the king was the most powerful woman in all the land. She sat at the king's right hand and could ask him for anything she wanted. People came to the queen mother to ask favors from the king, and we can, too. Hail, Holy Queen. Pray for us. Amen.

Day 3: Blessed Virgin Mary, because of your humility and obedience, God glorified you and made you Queen of Heaven. Teach us to be humble so that our hearts will be open to God's amazing plan for our lives. Each one of us is precious to God and precious to you, our mother. Rule us with your loving heart so that we can live lives of grace and purity like you. Amen.

Day 4: Holy Mary, Mother of God, you are always present wherever Jesus is with us in the Eucharist. You love and adore Jesus at the altar at Mass, and you pray for us to know him, to love him, and to serve him. You are very pleased with your children when we are **reverent** at Mass. Thank you for showing us that we should love Jesus in the Eucharist, no matter how difficult it might be to understand this great mystery. Amen.

Day 5: Sorrowful and Immaculate Heart of Mary, when Jesus was crucified, the Roman soldiers were very cruel and frightening. But you were very brave and stood by the cross, no matter how much they laughed and yelled at you. You brought Jesus strength to endure through your love and prayers. Help us to remember that when we suffer in any way, you are there with us, giving us courage the way you gave courage to Jesus. Amen.

Week 23:
Epiphany

*What gift will I give Jesus to show that I love him as my king,
my God, and my brother? (Choose something you own
that your parents will allow you to give away.)*

Vocabulary: homage, prostrated, scholars, ancient, Magi,
anoint

> *When Jesus was born in Bethlehem of Judea, in the days of
> King Herod, behold, magi from the east arrived in Jerusa-
> lem, saying, "Where is the newborn king of the Jews? We saw
> his star at its rising and have come to do him **homage**"....
> After their audience with the king they set out. And behold,
> the star that they had seen at its rising preceded them, until
> it came and stopped over the place where the child was.
> They were overjoyed at seeing the star, and on entering the
> house they saw the child with Mary his mother. They **pros-
> trated** themselves and did him homage. Then they opened
> their treasures and offered him gifts of gold, frankincense,
> and myrrh.*

> Matthew 2:1–2, 9–11

Day 1: Holy souls in purgatory, you are journeying to the shining gates of heaven, and some day you will be with Jesus, our
king, for all eternity. We offer our whole week to God for you—
our work, play, and learning—in solidarity with your purifica-
tion. Remind us that you are just as much a part of the Church
and the family of God as ever. Pray for us until we reach heaven,
too. Amen.

Day 2: Holy guardian angels, the Wise Men were **scholars** who studied the stars and the **ancient** prophecies. They worked hard to find God so they would be able to know him, love him, and serve him. Please help us learn as much as we can. Teach us to rejoice in the ways God speaks to us through the truth of the Bible, the glory of the stars, and the discoveries of science. Amen.

Day 3: Humble St. Joseph, the **Magi** brought gifts of gold, frankincense, and myrrh to Baby Jesus. The gold was a gift for a king; the frankincense was for praising and adoring God; and the myrrh was for **anoint**ing the dead. These amazing gifts showed that the Magi knew Baby Jesus was a king, that he was also God, and that he was also a human being who would die for our sins. Saint Joseph, pray that we will adore Jesus our king, our God, and our brother. Amen.

Day 4: Lord Jesus, You are our king, our God, and our brother. Our hearts are never truly happy until we trust you and invite you into our hearts. Even if we are too young to receive you in the Eucharist, help us receive you into our hearts. It is very mysterious, but in the holy Mass, you come to us looking and tasting like bread and wine. You give yourself to us completely. Help us to give ourselves back to you. Amen.

Day 5: Jesus, the bright star of Bethlehem showed the Magi how to find you. Our beloved Church is like a bright star in the world, leading people to find you, too. Help us to love the Church and to love the pope, our bishops, and all priests and religious. Help us to appreciate the sign that they are to the world, since they have given up everything to follow you. Bless all the bright stars who lead us to you. Amen.

Week 24:
The Holy Family

What is special about home?
What more can we do to be a gift to our families?

...Behold, the angel of the Lord appeared to Joseph in a dream and said, "Rise, take the child and his mother, flee to Egypt, and stay there until I tell you. Herod is going to search for the child to destroy him. Joseph rose and took the child and his mother by night and departed for Egypt. He stayed there until the death of Herod, that what the Lord had said through the prophet might be fulfilled, "Out of Egypt I called my son."

Matthew 2:13–15

Day 1: Lord, help us to be sensitive to anyone in our midst who might be from another country or new to our town. It can be very hard for anyone to leave behind their relatives and friends to move to a new place, but sometimes that is what God asks of us. Thank you for always being with us, no matter where we travel or live or go to school. Bless all who are new to this place, and bless us when we make them feel welcome. Amen.

Day 2: Holy Spirit, when we listen to you, we receive guidance that helps us have the best lives possible. When we are attentive to the teachings we receive through the Church, our teachers, and our parents, you strengthen us for whatever journeys and adventures are ahead. When we place our trust in you, your protection is all around us. Thank you for loving us in every moment of our lives. Amen.

Day 3: St. Joseph, your prayers are very powerful as you watch over the Church and our families. Help us to appreciate our own homes and families, even though they are not perfect. Some people don't have homes at all, and some people don't have a family to love them. Please keep praying for us every day to become holy and generous in the way we live so that others will experience the love of Christ through us. Amen.

Day 4: Lord Jesus, it can seem strange to us that you are really present in the Eucharist—not far away in some other time and place. The host and the Precious Blood look, taste, and smell like ordinary bread and wine. But you told us that you are the Bread of Life, and you taught the apostles to share this gift with others, just as our priests do today. Help us to believe in you, Lord. Feed our hungry hearts with your holy presence. Amen.

Day 5: Lord, you never leave us alone because you love us so much, even when we feel like there is no one there. You live in our souls, and you are all around us in the beauty of nature, the love of our families and friends, and the precious teachings of Holy Mother Church. Thank you for helping us to know you through prayer and service, through the Bible, and through the sacraments. Where you are present, we are truly home. Amen.

SECTION SIX

All Are Welcome

Week 25:
Witness

Have you ever felt embarrassed to try something you've never done before? Sometimes God asks us to take a risk and learn a new skill so his light can shine through us.

You are the light of the world. A city set on a mountain cannot be hidden. Nor do they light a lamp and then put it under a bushel basket; it is set on a lampstand, where it gives light to all in the house. Just so, your light must shine before others, that they may see your good deeds and glorify your heavenly Father.

Matthew 5:14–16

Day 1: Come Holy Spirit, fill our hearts with courage. You speak to our hearts of your holy love, but sometimes we have a hard time sharing that message with others. Inspire and bless us so we can be fearless followers of Jesus Christ. Through our hard work, our kindness, and our willingness to forgive, we shine brightly and bring the presence of Christ into our everyday lives. Come, Holy Spirit, help us shine. Amen.

Day 2: Blessed companion, my guardian angel, never leave my side. Pray for me each day, as I learn to be a follower of Jesus Christ. To be a Christian is to love. But sometimes I feel angry or upset by the behavior of other people. Sometimes I'm confused and disappointed with myself. Remind me of God's divine mercy. God loves us no matter what, so I should never be discouraged by my sins or the sins of others. Amen.

Day 3: God, you have made us in your image. Like you, we
in a community of love. You are Father, Son, and Holy Spirit, a
family full of purity, mercy, and joy. Strengthen us so we can lift
each other up and help each other shine in our families, church-
es, and schools. When we focus on what is good in each other
and praise the people around us, we start to see people the way
God sees them. Amen.

Day 4: Lord, help us to see everyone with the light of your love.
Your beauty can seem hidden in the Blessed Sacrament, but you
really are present in all your glory. It can be hard for us to see
the beauty and glory in the souls all around us. People don't always show the light and love of God in their words and actions,
and we don't always look for the best in each other. Bless our
eyes so we may see what is good in every person. Amen.

Day 5: Sacred Heart of Jesus, bless all those who teach us,
whether they are schoolteachers, catechists, parents, grandparents, coaches, or others who sacrifice their time and energy for
us. Help us pay close attention to them because your messages
of love are found in every lesson. Thank you, Jesus, for loving us
through the people who work so hard to help us shine with your
light. Amen.

Week 26:
Works of Mercy

Do you have any toys, books, or clothing
you could give to the poor?

_____

He will place the sheep on his right and the goats on his left.
Then the king will say to those on his right, "Come, you who
are blessed by my Father. Inherit the kingdom prepared for
you from the foundation of the world. For I was hungry and
you gave me food, I was thirsty and you gave me drink, a
stranger and you welcomed me, naked and you clothed me,
ill and you cared for me, in prison and you visited me." Then
the righteous will answer him and say, "Lord, when did we
see you hungry and feed you, or thirsty and give you drink?
When did we see you a stranger and welcome you, or naked
and clothe you? When did we see you ill or in prison, and
visit you?" And the king will say to them in reply, "Amen, I
say to you, whatever you did for one of these least brothers
of mine, you did for me."

Matthew 25:33–40

Day 1: Dear God, we know that you dearly love the holy souls
in purgatory and that you want us to pray for them every day.
They are hungry and thirsty for your mercy, as they wait to be
purified of their sins and clothed with your glory. Through your
grace, our prayers help them join the joy of heaven more quickly.
Remind us to pray for them, and ask them to pray for us until we
come into your presence, too. Amen.

Day 2: Lord, every day there is someone you are asking us to love. Sometimes it is a person hungry for a smile or a kind word. Sometimes it is someone who needs our help to understand a lesson or learn a skill. You have been so generous to each of us, giving us gifts, like our talents and abilities, that we are meant to share. Whenever we are kind to anyone, we are kind to you. Thank you for letting us serve you, Jesus. Amen.

Day 3: Lord, you are present in every human soul. Help us to remember your presence in each other, as we spend time together today. When we look into each other's eyes and listen to each other's voices, help us to see you and hear you. Give us the grace to treat every person as we would treat you if you were in front of us. Lord, thank you for being with us. Amen.

Day 4: Dear Jesus, you are so humble and kind. It's amazing that you are really present in the holy Eucharist at Mass. Give us a hunger to receive you in holy Communion, and make our souls thirsty to share your love with others. Even if we are not able to receive communion please come into our souls and nourish us spiritually. Make us humble and kind like you. Thank you, Jesus. Amen.

Day 5: Jesus, your sacred heart burns with love for us. Help us to see that love is more than just a feeling; it is an action. Doing what is right, no matter how hard it is—that's love. Being willing to share what little we have—that's love. Speaking up when we see someone being hurt in any way—that's love. Jesus, fill our hearts with love and the courage to use that love to help others. We praise you for your goodness. Amen.

Week 27:
Unity

When is it hard to be patient with others?

I, then, a prisoner for the Lord, urge you to live in a manner worthy of the call you have received, with all humility and gentleness, with patience, bearing with one another through love, striving to preserve the unity of the spirit through the bond of peace: one body and one Spirit, as you were also called to the one hope of your call; one Lord, one faith, one baptism; one God and Father of all, who is over all and through all and in all.

Ephesians 4:1–6

Day 1: Dear God, you are always so good to us. Even when we aren't sure how to pray, you understand us perfectly. You love us even when we can't love ourselves. Fill our hearts with your mercy and make it overflow into the hearts of others. Teach us how to love even the most difficult people and help us to forgive them and ourselves. You are Father, Son, and Holy Spirit, a perfect unity of love and communion. Help us to live in the unity of the Holy Spirit now and forever. Amen.

Day 2: Most patient Lord, bless us with patience and teach us the value of accepting each other with all our quirks and weaknesses. We are sinners, all of us, so we should never point a finger at the faults of others unless they are causing harm or danger to someone. There isn't anyone in the whole world you don't love. Help us remember we are all one body in Christ and need your help every day to be better than we were yesterday. Amen.

Day 3: Dear Lord, you are God and Father to all of us here, and you are God and Father to everyone in the world. It is amazing to think of the billions of people in different countries around the globe. They may speak a different language, have different beliefs, look different, and eat different foods, but each one is precious to you. Help us remember, most loving Father, that we can look into our own hearts to find you because you choose to be with us always. We can look into the face of anyone and catch a glimpse of your holy presence. Amen.

Day 4: Dear Jesus, Prince of Peace, when we are frightened or upset, worried or in a bad mood, please give us the grace to offer that suffering to you. You offered yourself on the cross to save us from our sins and bring us peace. When we join our sufferings to your sufferings, our little sacrifice of love becomes holy and helps change the world. You are the source of all peace. Help us to be peaceful, even when we are having a rough day. Amen.

Day 5: Sacred Heart of Jesus, your heart is infinitely loving. There is no person and no problem that is too much for you to handle. You are so happy when we pray and ask for your help. The more we think about your heart, the more we become like you. Jesus, bless us in this moment and help us to remember your sacred heart throughout the day. Make our hearts burn with love for you and make us strong to do your will. Amen.

Week 28:
Inclusion

*How will you share God's love with someone else today?
Can you invite someone new to eat a snack with you?*

Vocabulary: exalt, lame, popular, disability

*For everyone who **exalts** himself will be humbled, but the one who humbles himself will be exalted. Then he said to the host who invited him, "When you hold a lunch or a dinner, do not invite your friends or your brothers or your relatives or your wealthy neighbors, in case they may invite you back and you have repayment. Rather, when you hold a banquet, invite the poor, the crippled, the **lame**, the blind; blessed indeed will you be because of their inability to repay you. For you will be repaid at the resurrection of the righteous."*

Luke 14:11–14

Day 1: Holy Spirit, grant that we may be humble enough to receive every grace and blessing from you today and then share it with others in some way. The holy souls in purgatory need our prayers and our sacrifices. Every time we offer a little prayer or do our work cheerfully for them, they come closer to entering heaven. Teach us, Lord, to be humble and kind so that the riches of heaven will be ours to share with everyone we meet. Amen.

Day 2: Lord Jesus, important and **popular** people sometimes got upset with you because you hung out with people who were not important or popular. You would sit and share a nice meal with men and women who didn't believe the same things you did. Some of them were made fun of and excluded for being poor or sick, or for making wrong choices. But you loved them all, and many of them gave their hearts to you and became healthy, happy, and holy. Help us to love everybody, dear Jesus. Amen.

Day 3: Dear God, you are all good and all holy. You are gentle and humble. You accept everyone and love everyone. Help us to be grateful for our friendships and our families. The best way to say "thank you, God" for these precious gifts is to share them. Teach us to open our minds and hearts to new friendships with people we would not normally talk to or play with. They are placed in our lives for a reason. Help us to be courageous and reach out to them, loving Lord. Thank you for blessing our efforts. Amen.

Day 4: Jesus, when you were arrested and handed over to the Roman soldiers to be hurt and killed, your best friends all ran away. They were scared, like we sometimes are, so they hid from the pain and the danger. Jesus, when we feel alone and scared, help us remember that you never leave us. You would do anything for us, which is why you gave your life for us on the cross. Bless us with courage, faith, and hope so our lives will fill up with love and help heal the world. Amen.

Day 5: Sacred Heart of Jesus, there is room in your heart for everyone. You especially love those who are suffering because they carry a heavy cross, as you did. When we meet people who are different from us—those with a **disability** or those who struggle in any way—please remind us that they are extra-special to you. Help us treat everyone with great affection and kindness. Whatever we do to others, we do to you. Thank you for inviting us to love you by loving others. Amen.

Week 29:
Reconciliation

When our feelings are hurt, what actions show forgiveness?
How do we show others that we are sorry for our mistakes?

Vocabulary: pride, absolution

But if we walk in the light as he is in the light, then we have
fellowship with one another, and the blood of his Son Jesus
cleanses us from all sin. If we say, "We are without sin," we
deceive ourselves, and the truth is not in us. If we acknowl-
edge our sins, he is faithful and just and will forgive our sins
and cleanse us from every wrongdoing.

1 John 1:7–9

Day 1: Holy Spirit, every day you have bright, shining gifts of
grace to give us, but sometimes our **pride** gets in the way and
we choose to walk in darkness. You want to share your glory and
power with us, but when we insist on sinning and doing things
our own way, we turn away from you and miss the chance to
share in those heavenly gifts. Give us the grace to love you more
than we love anything else so that we will avoid sin and walk in
the light of your love. Amen.

Day 2: Dear Jesus, everybody makes mistakes. But when we admit we're wrong, say we're sorry, and try to do better, you are
so happy with us. You don't even want to remember our sins
once you have forgiven them. If we are old enough, please give
us the courage and the wisdom to ask our parents to take us to

reconciliation so we can confess our sins to a priest and receive **absolution**. If we are not old enough, give us the grace to ask for your forgiveness in our hearts. Amen.

Day 3: Dear God, you are all that is good and truthful, joyful and sweet. When we confess our sins and do our best to do better, you bless our families and our friendships. You pour out your gifts of love into our lives when we humbly admit we are not perfect. You always bless us for doing the right thing, and you bless us greatly when we are sorry for doing the wrong thing. Thank you for shining the light of your love into our hearts. Amen.

Day 4: Jesus, when we receive you in the holy Eucharist or even just pray reverently during the Mass, you brighten our souls with your heavenly light. Your sacrifice on the cross brought healing and blessing to our souls, and that sacrifice is truly present to us at Mass. There is great power in the Eucharist because the bread and wine become your Body, Blood, Soul, and Divinity. Thank you for this precious, healing gift of love. Help us to always treasure you at Mass, Lord Jesus. Amen.

Day 5: Lord Jesus, when you opened the gates of heaven through your sacrifice on the cross, you showed us that our crosses are blessings, too. You taught us not to be afraid of suffering so that when we have to work extra hard or wait patiently for something good to happen, we know that you are working powerfully in our lives to bless the world. Jesus, the more we accept our crosses and place our trust in you, the stronger and more heroic we become, and the more we are able to fight the temptation to sin. Jesus, through your gifts of grace, make us holy. Amen.

SECTION SEVEN

Lent

Week 30:
Faith

*What sacrifice of prayer or service will you offer to God
to save souls this Lent?*

Vocabulary: despair, heritage, distress, fasting, heroine

> *Your strength is not in numbers, nor does your might depend upon the powerful. You are God of the lowly, helper of those of little account, supporter of the weak, protector of those in **despair**, savior of those without hope. Please, please, God of my father, God of the **heritage** of Israel, Master of heaven and earth, Creator of the waters, King of all you have created, hear my prayer!*

Judith 9:11–12

> *My Lord, you alone are our King. Help me, who am alone and have no help but you, for I am taking my life in my hand....Make yourself known in the time of our **distress** and give me courage, King of gods and Ruler of every power.*

Esther C: 14–15, 23

Day 1: Lord God, Judith was a respected judge in Israel who defeated a whole army with her great faith and courage. She prepared to meet her enemies by **fasting** and praying. Queen Esther, an orphaned Jewish girl who was chosen to marry a pagan king, defeated thousands of enemies. Thank you for these holy **heroine**s of the Bible who remind us that when we pray and make sacrifices, you bless us and help us triumph over danger and sin. Amen.

Day 2: Dearest guardian angel, help me remember you are always at my side, praying for me and helping me to be strong in faith, hope, and love. When I trust in God and pray with my whole heart for those who need help, God blesses those prayers and brings his love and power to our lives. With prayer and sacrifice, I can become a holy warrior, too. Holy angel, never stop praying for me, as I learn, little by little, what it means to be a soldier in the great army of God's love. Amen.

Day 3: Lord, when we pray with faith in your holy power, you are pleased with us. Fill our hearts with confidence in your love, and help us to see the ways you answer our prayers. You speak to us through our lessons, the books we read, the Bible readings we hear, and through the love of people. You even speak to us in the beauty of nature and in the quiet of our own hearts. Thank you, Lord, for always answering our prayers. Amen.

Day 4: Lord Jesus, you lived your life with such gentleness and compassion. You healed the blind and the lame and even raised the dead. You worked very hard, traveling all over the Holy Land, serving, teaching, and working miracles. Even though you are God, you knew how important it was to take time for prayer every day. Sometimes you even prayed throughout the night. Your heavenly Father was very pleased, sending you countless miracles of love to share with us. Help us pray hard every day and see what gifts of grace God will send us. Amen.

Day 5: Sacred Heart of Jesus, you are almighty, glorious, and powerful, but you love to work miracles of grace through the small, weak people of this world. That is how we know that it is your power, not ours, making our lives so much better. We need you, Lord, and we are so grateful that when we come to you in humble prayer, you share your glory and power with us, and you allow us to be channels of that love and power to others. Amen.

Week 31:
Prayer

When you pray the prayer that Jesus taught us,
do you think of God here with us right now?

Vocabulary: hallowed, debtors, vast

> *Your Father knows what you need before you ask him. This is how you are to pray: Our Father in heaven, **hallowed** be your name, your kingdom come, your will be done, on earth as in heaven. Give us today our daily bread; and forgive us our debts, as we forgive our **debtors**; and do not subject us to the final test, but deliver us from the evil one.*
>
> Matthew 6:8–13

Day 1: Lord, when we make the sign of the cross, you draw us into your presence and protect our hearts from darkness. When we pray each day, help us remember that we are standing before your holy throne and you are really with us. It is holy and powerful to come to you with all our needs. It is a joy to our hearts to praise you for all your love and glory, power and mercy. Amen.

Day 2: Lord God, in your amazing generosity, you have created us to be part of a vast family of souls known as the Church. As members of the Church on earth, we are still praying and fighting against our sins. Those who have already died can be part of the Church in Purgatory. These souls need our prayers to help them get to heaven. Those triumphant souls in heaven—the saints—pray for us night and day until we enter heaven, too. Thank you for this beautiful family. Amen.

Day 3: Lord Jesus, you are always ready to forgive our sins. When you taught the apostles to pray, you told them to ask God to forgive them their sins as much as they forgave others. Bless us, Lord, with the ability to really forgive people when they hurt us. When we forgive, we are forgiven, too. Amen.

Day 4: Dear God, you are perfect and wise, and you know what is best for us. Sometimes we feel like you aren't listening to our prayers because we don't get what we want. It can be painful for us to wait and see what your holy will is going to be. Help us to trust you with all our hearts so that when we pray, "Thy will be done," we are at peace, knowing that you will do what is best for our souls. Thank you for loving us, Lord. Amen.

Day 5: Sacred Heart of Jesus, you were born into a poor family and worked hard all your life. Help us trust that, even when it seems other people have everything and we have nothing, you are with us, loving us. The gift of your friendship is the greatest treasure of all because you bring us the true riches of heaven: faith, hope, and love. Make us peaceful and joyful, and grant that other people's prayers may be answered through our acts of kindness. Amen.

Week 32:
Fasting

*Can you think of a way to give a gift to someone else
without that person knowing it?*

_____

Vocabulary: fortitude

When you fast, do not look gloomy like the hypocrites. They neglect their appearance, so that they may appear to others to be fasting. Amen, I say to you, they have received their reward. But when you fast, anoint your head and wash your face, so that you may not appear to others to be fasting, except to your Father who is hidden. And your Father who sees what is hidden will repay you.

Matthew 6:16–18

Day 1: Dear Holy Spirit, you are so comforting and wise. Help us to be happy to give up something for Lent. When we sacrifice something and offer it to you, you strengthen us to resist temptations of every kind. With that self-control comes joy and peace. Bless us with the **fortitude** to keep trying, even though it's hard to give up the things we enjoy. The suffering we experience is a way of saying "thank you" to Jesus for his suffering on the cross, and it's a good way of atoning for our sins. Come and strengthen us, Holy Spirit. Amen.

Day 2: Dearest angel guardian, you give yourself totally to God, and you watch over me, day and night. Help me to be selfless and heroic like you. I want to stop complaining about the little things that bother me, but it's hard. Would you please ask God to send me special graces today so I can be joyful throughout the day? I ask this with confidence in your powerful intercession and your loving devotion to the good of my soul. Amen.

Day 3: Brave St. Joseph, so often you had to do things that were hard, but you never hesitated to do God's will. As soon as you were sure what God wanted, you jumped right in. Pray for us so we will learn how to pray and listen for God's guidance in our lives and not be afraid to do what is right. When we learn to answer God's call, we find our best, most fulfilling path to heaven. Thank you for your prayers, holy St. Joseph. Amen.

Day 4: Dear Jesus, your most holy presence is hidden in the Eucharist. It's amazing how humble you are. You don't ask for anything but our love in return for the amazing gift of your Body, Blood, Soul, and Divinity. To be more like you, we can hide some of our sacrifices this Lent. Whether it is giving up a special treat, time watching TV, or using our phones, help us to be cheerful and more willing than usual to help others. Lord Jesus, we want to be more like you. Amen.

Day 5: Sacred Heart of Jesus, you shower us with graces and blessings when we make even a small effort to be kind and selfless. Help us to appreciate everything that other people do for us, the same way you appreciate our little sacrifices. The more we look for the good in others, the more we will see. And the more good we see, the happier we'll be, and the more we will come close to your heart, sweet Jesus. Amen.

Week 33:
Almsgiving

*What kind of almsgiving (giving money, time, or labor)
is hardest for you? Do it for Jesus today.*

Vocabulary: abounds

*[Jesus] sat down opposite the treasury and observed how
the crowd put money into the treasury. Many rich people
put in large sums. A poor widow also came and put in two
small coins worth a few cents. Calling his disciples to himself, he said to them, "Amen, I say to you, this poor widow
put in more than all the other contributors to the treasury.
For they have all contributed from their surplus wealth,
but she, from her poverty, has contributed all she had, her
whole livelihood."*

Mark 12:41–44

Day 1: Lord, your generosity is all around us. It speaks to us
through the love of our families, the riches of our education,
the beauty of nature, and especially in the sacraments. We want
to be generous, but often we feel like we have nothing to give.
Show us how we can offer our small talents and treasures to you
with a generous spirit. Grant us the grace to put people before
things and to be joyful in sharing what we have. Amen.

Day 2: God, you can see right into our hearts. You know we are sometimes anxious. Please fill our hearts to the brim with your love so we will never again be caught in the trap of worrying about the future. When you touch our hearts and ask us to be generous, help us to trust that you will provide everything we truly need. When we trust in you, we find true peace and lasting joy. We praise you, our God. Amen.

Day 3: Lord Jesus, when you watched the people putting their offerings into the temple treasury, you could see who was really making a sacrifice and who was just showing off. Please give us the grace to share what we have with a sincere heart, and show us the many fruits of our sacrifices. We know that when we are generous with others, you bless our charity and your grace **abounds**. We offer all things in your holy name, Lord Jesus. Amen.

Day 4: Jesus, when you taught your disciples, you were always respectful. You are God and they were only simple men, but you didn't treat them like they weren't smart enough to understand important lessons. You were patient and kind, and you gave them the chance to learn from you and become better people. Give us the grace to always treat everyone with respect and to encourage each other to be the best we can be. Amen.

Day 5: Lord Jesus, you never owned very much here on earth. You are God, so you could have made yourself a wealthy king or a powerful general. Yet you chose to be a poor carpenter who worked very hard for very little money, and then you left your home behind to teach us about your heavenly kingdom. Thank you for showing us that a rich life is a life that is given for others. We praise you for your spirit of love and sacrifice, Lord Jesus. Amen.

Week 34:
Service

Talk about a time you sacrificed something for another person and were surprised at how blessed you felt.

——————————————

Give and gifts will be given to you; a good measure, packed together, shaken down, and overflowing, will be poured into your lap. For the measure with which you measure will in return be measured out to you.

Luke 6:38

Day 1: Holy Spirit, you are always with us, speaking to our hearts and teaching us to love. The holy souls in purgatory need our prayers and works to help them get to heaven. Please remind us throughout the day that any time we offer our work or play time for the holy souls, we help to fill heaven with shouts and songs of joy. Amen.

Day 2: Holy guardian angels, sometimes we fear sharing what we have, especially our time. Help us to be happy to give ourselves in service to each other. Open our eyes to the many possibilities all around us at home, at school, and at church. Who is it that God would like me to help today? I ask for the grace to see the needs of others and the courage to step forward and offer myself in service. When I serve, I love as God loves. Amen.

Day 3: St. Joseph, please pray for our families so we may see clearly that every act of loving service brings an abundance of blessings into our lives. The family is the best place to learn to love as God loves, with a willingness to forget ourselves and think only of what is best for those we love. Inspire us, dear St. Joseph, to be happy to sacrifice our comforts to bring hope to others and holiness to our own souls. Amen

Day 4: Jesus, thank you for giving yourself to us in the holy Eucharist. When I look at the host, I am amazed at how humble you are. Your most holy presence in the Blessed Sacrament is so quiet and hidden, and yet all your glory and power is offered to us as food for our souls. Help me to serve others without making a fuss and give me great joy every time I do a kind act in secret. Having my good deed be invisible makes me more like you. I love you, Jesus. Amen.

Day 5: Sacred Heart of Jesus, love in action helps to heal the world of its sorrows, its pain, and its hunger. Whenever we listen to you and reach out to someone in need, we are loving not only that person but also you, great and holy God. Jesus, you said that whatever we do to others we do to you, so give us wisdom and inspire us to find ways to help everyone in our lives. Amen.

Week 35:
Holy Week

Who is the bravest person you know?

_____

Yet it was our pain that he bore, our sufferings he endured. We thought of him as stricken, struck down by God and afflicted, But he was pierced for our sins, crushed for our iniquity. He bore the punishment that makes us whole, by his wounds we were healed.

Isaiah 53:4–5

Day 1: Lord Jesus, on Palm Sunday, we raised our palm branches and waved them for joy. More than 2,000 years ago, you rode into Jerusalem on the back of a donkey, and crowds of people waved their palm branches and shouted, "Hosanna to the King!" When we wave our palms, we welcome you into our hearts and enthrone you in our souls. Help us remember that you are always with us, that you are our king, as well as our brother, and that you will never abandon us. Amen.

Day 2: Dearest Jesus, help us understand how your sufferings set us free from the bondage of our sins. We were prisoners of our own sins, but your generous heart was able to open the doors of the prison to set us free. It wasn't easy. For evil to be defeated and the gates of heaven to be opened, you gave yourself as a sacrifice. Jesus, we love you. Thank you for loving us so much. Amen.

Day 3: Lord Jesus, when you washed the feet of the apostles, you showed them that a truly great leader is willing to humble himself and serve others. Your example shows me that if I want to be my best self and live the most wonderful life possible, I should look for ways to be helpful to others. My life is precious to you, dear Jesus, and I know you have a beautiful plan for my life. Give me the courage to help you change the world through love in action. Amen.

Day 4: Precious Lord Jesus, at the Last Supper you taught the apostles. "This is my Body," you said, holding up the bread. "This is my Blood," you said, holding up the cup of wine. When the priest says these same words at Mass, the bread and wine are transformed through your mysterious power and become your Body, Blood, Soul, and Divinity. This is infinitely powerful food for our souls. Jesus, you are amazing and generous. Thank you for always being with us at Mass and in our hearts. We love you. Amen.

Day 5: Dear Jesus, since you offered your suffering to save us and you want us to be like you, we can also offer our sufferings to save others. When I am sad, tired, or in pain, help me to remember to pray, "Jesus, I am on the cross with you. I love you." Help me to offer my pain for all the people of the world who do not yet know you and do not yet love you. We are members of your body, Jesus, so we can help to save the world, too. Amen.

SECTION EIGHT

Easter

Week 36:
Easter

*Have you ever been sad right before
you found out something wonderful?*

Vocabulary: tomb, miraculous, sacred

*But Mary [of Magdala] stayed outside the **tomb** weeping. And as she wept, she bent over into the tomb and saw two angels in white sitting there, one at the head and one at the feet where the body of Jesus had been. And they said to her, "Woman, why are you weeping?" She said to them, "They have taken my Lord, and I don't know where they laid him." When she had said this, she turned around and saw Jesus there, but did not know it was Jesus....Jesus said to her, "Mary!" She turned and said to him in Hebrew, "Rabbouni," which means Teacher. Jesus said to her, "...go to my brothers and tell them, 'I am going to my Father and your Father, to my God and your God.'" Mary of Magdala went and announced to the disciples, "I have seen the Lord," and what he told her.*

John 20:11–14, 16–18

Day 1: Holy God, your only Son was willing to pay the price for our sins. Through the wounds that he suffered, he defeated evil and opened the gates of heaven for all of us. Give us the grace to believe in your Son's **miraculous** resurrection so that we will never be afraid of sickness, injury, rejection, or death. Give us courage, Lord, to accept our crosses with love and trust in your power to bring good out of everything. Amen.

Day 2: Holy angels, you guarded the **sacred** tomb of Jesus, even after he rose from the dead. You witnessed his glorious resurrection and then waited for St. Mary of Magdala to arrive at the tomb. What a blessing that all God's children are surrounded by angels all the days of our lives. Pray for us without ceasing, dear guardians, watching over our souls and preparing them to receive the risen Jesus. Amen.

Day 3: St. Joseph, how hard it must have been for you and the Blessed Mother to raise your beloved Son, knowing that he must suffer and die for our sins. Yet, you trusted in the will of God, knowing that the resurrection of Jesus would be the most powerful event in history. Thank you for praying for our families and classmates, St. Joseph, and for everyone we place in your powerful and tender loving care. Amen.

Day 4: Dear Jesus, it's sometimes hard for us to understand that you are truly present in holy Communion. That small circle of bread looks so plain and ordinary. Help us, through the intercession of St. Mary of Magdala, to believe that it is really you who appear to us in such an unexpected way. Mary saw you resurrected and then ran out to tell the disciples the joyful news. Fill us with a courageous and lasting joy so our lives will announce your presence to everyone we meet. Amen.

Day 5: Sacred Heart of Jesus, you are the greatest teacher of all time. Through your teachings, stories, and miracles you changed the course of human history. You brought your radiant light to a dark world. You have taught us to hope in you at all times. You overcame death, Lord Jesus. Thank you, precious risen Lord, for the gracious gift of your resurrection, your victory over sin and death. Amen.

Week 37:
Divine Mercy

What do you think the prophet Micah means when he says that God takes our sins and casts them "into the depths of the sea?"

Vocabulary: remnant, iniquities

> *Who is a God like you, who removes guilt and pardons sin for the **remnant** of his inheritance; Who does not persist in anger forever, but instead delights in mercy, And will again have compassion on us, treading underfoot our **iniquities**? You will cast into the depths of the sea all our sins; You will show faithfulness to Jacob, and loyalty to Abraham, As you have sworn to our ancestors from days of old.*
>
> Micah 7:18–20

Day 1: Lord, the holy souls in purgatory are our neighbors, friends, and family members who are already on their way to heaven. Jesus, bathe them in your beautiful mercy, wash away every stain of sin from their souls and welcome them into your gentle radiance. Today we offer all our work and prayers for these holy souls, and we trust that they will pray for us until we enter heaven, too. Amen.

Day 2: Dear guardian angels, help us grow in the virtue of mercy so we will be quick to forgive others their faults and even their sins against us. Show us the best in others and the best in ourselves. God is the source of all that is good, true, and beautiful. When we look for the best in each other, it's like looking into the face of God. Amen.

Day 3: St. Joseph, because you trusted in divine mercy, angels appeared to you in dreams, bringing God's words of comfort and command. You believed those words of comfort. You obeyed God's commands. Pray for us, St. Joseph, that we will be more like you, trusting and obeying God all the days of our lives. Amen.

Day 4: Adorable Jesus, present in the most Blessed Sacrament, you are always kind and good. You love us more than we can imagine, with infinite affection and mercy, even though we make many mistakes. Have mercy on us, Lord. Make your divine mercy grow in our hearts so that we will become like you: full of love, compassion, and forgiveness. Amen.

Day 5: Lord, it has been a busy week full of work, friendship, joys, and sorrows. Please help us to look back over this week and see the many ways your mercy touched our lives. Each time someone was kind to us, someone forgave us, someone helped us, or someone tried to see the good in us, we were touched by your merciful heart. Help us to be merciful to others, living our lives with great gentleness and joy. Amen.

Week 38:
Joy and Peace

Why does the Bible tell us to be joyful and not give in to anxiety?

Vocabulary: petition, salvation

> *Rejoice in the Lord always. I shall say it again: rejoice! Your kindness should be known to all. The Lord is near. Have no anxiety at all, but in everything, by prayer and **petition**, with thanksgiving, make your requests known to God. Then the peace of God that surpasses all understanding will guard your hearts and minds in Christ Jesus.*

Philippians 4:4–7

Day 1: Come, Holy Spirit, fill our hearts with the joy of our **salvation**. Everyone has moments of sadness, loneliness, or fear, so make us bright, shining messengers of your holy joy to the world. Inspire us to do good works, even if no one here on earth will see them or thank us for them. We know that you see all things, Lord, and that you are pleased when we bring happiness to others. Jesus is risen. Alleluia! Amen.

Day 2: Holy angels, help us to count our blessings today, and to do everything in a spirit of gratitude. As we work and play, help us to thank God for the great gift of our lives, our education, our family, our friends, the beauty of nature, and Holy Mother Church. We want to bring greater glory to God in all we do and to make our lives a gift to the most Holy Trinity: Father, Son, and Holy Spirit. Amen.

Day 3: Lord Jesus, Prince of Peace, we bring all our cares and questions to you, knowing that you can see right into our hearts. Before we can even think of what to pray for, you already know everything we need. You see us so clearly, Jesus. But you love it when we talk to you; so from now on, any time I am worried or anxious, I am going to talk it over with you and rest in your holy peace. Amen.

Day 4: Blessed Mother Mary, you must have been very surprised when the angel first appeared to you to tell you that you would be the mother of Jesus, our Lord. Knowing that your beautiful Son would one day die for our sins must have been very sad. But you always trusted in God's plan for your life so that even during times of suffering, you carried the peace of God in your heart. Help us to trust in Jesus. Amen.

Day 5: Sacred Heart of Jesus, you look deep into our hearts and see the beauty there. You see our kindness, our forgiveness, our joys and sorrows—and our sins, too. Yet, you love us just as we are and you bless us for sharing your love with others. Help us to show our faith in your merciful love by sharing a smile with someone in need today. Amen.

Week 39:
Life in Christ

What does the expression "God is love" mean to you?

_____

For this reason I kneel before the Father, from whom every family in heaven and on earth is named, that he may grant you in accord with the riches of his glory to be strengthened with power through his Spirit in the inner self, and that Christ may dwell in your hearts through faith; that you, rooted and grounded in love, may have strength to comprehend with all the holy ones what is the breadth and length and height and depth, and to know the love of Christ that surpasses knowledge, so that you may be filled with all the fullness of God.

Ephesians 3:14–19

Day 1: Come, loving Holy Spirit, touch our hearts and minds with your holy power and help us to grow in wisdom and understanding. We want to know God so we can love him and serve him with all our hearts. We want to be strong in faith so we can help lead other souls to heaven. We want to be pleasing to God so we can enter heaven ourselves some day. Strengthen us to live in holiness and joy. Amen.

Day 2: Dear Lord, you created the whole universe, so you understand every mystery. From the farthest reaches of the universe to the tiniest cells and atoms of our own bodies, you love the truth, goodness, and beauty of your whole creation. Thank you for sharing your knowledge with us through the hard work of our parents and teachers. We praise you for this opportunity to learn more about our beautiful world. Amen.

Day 3: Heavenly Father, you have given each of us gifts: families, talents, work, friendships, and learning experiences that will help us find the holy and exciting path you have created for our lives. Some of us will be saintly priests or religious brothers or sisters; others will remain single in order to serve you in a special way; and others will marry and raise holy families for the greater glory of God. Thank you for the great adventure of our lives, Lord. In all that is good, we find you. Amen.

Day 4: Dear Jesus, you teach us in so many ways. You are all good and totally loving. Your love lifts up our hearts and minds and fills them with hope. Thank you for all the people you have placed in our lives who spread your love by sharing your knowledge with us. Thank you for our parents and grandparents, our pastors and teachers, and our coaches and other leaders. The good they do comes from you. Amen.

Day 5: Dear Mary, most pure, you are filled up completely with God's presence. He has given you perfect wisdom and granted you the power to shower down graces into our souls. Grant us the wisdom to ask for those graces every day. Ask God to open our hearts to receive the graces we need most—especially the ones we don't know about. We love you, Blessed Mother. Thank you for your prayers for us. Amen.

Week 40:
Reverence

*What are some ways we are strong
when others think we are weak?*

Vocabulary: bestow, sanctuary

*[Jesus] humbled himself, becoming obedient to death, even
death on a cross. Because of this, God greatly exalted him
and **bestow**ed on him the name that is above every name,
that at the name of Jesus every knee should bend, of those
in heaven and on earth and under the earth, and every
tongue confess that Jesus Christ is Lord, to the glory of God
the Father.*

Philippians 2:8–11

Day 1: Holy Spirit, inspire us with a deep love and reverence
for Jesus in the Blessed Sacrament. Help us to kneel in church
with great love, knowing that we are in the presence of the most
high king of the universe. Help us to pray throughout the day in
the quiet **sanctuary** of our hearts, where Jesus waits with joy to
speak with us. Amen.

Day 2: Dear Jesus, you have shared your authority with the good
adults in our lives, so when we obey our parents and teachers,
we give honor to you. We understand that not all adults have the
Spirit of God in their hearts, but those who love us and protect
us are doing your holy work. Please help us to appreciate their
sacrifices and honor them out of love for you. Amen.

Day 3: Dear Jesus, when we treat others with kindness and respect, we honor you. When we share our food, help someone with their work, cheer up someone who is sad, or control our temper when others make mistakes, we love and honor you. You have sacrificed everything out of love for us, Lord, even though we are sinners. Please help us to love as you do, remembering that you don't wait for us to deserve your love. You just love. Amen.

Day 4: Most Holy Trinity, your holy presence is all around us, in all of nature, in the beauty of heaven, and deep in our souls. You are so powerful and perfect, we can't imagine how great you are. You choose to be with us at all times, and you invite us to come and live in heaven with you forever. Send your spirit, Lord, to inspire us to praise you all the days of our lives. Thank you for giving us the grace to love and serve you. Amen.

Day 5: Sweet Jesus, sometimes it's hard for us to understand the virtue of humility. When you humbled yourself to die on the cross for us, you paid the price for our sins. You didn't have to do that. You could have said "no" to the Father. But you loved us so much that you became small and human, like us, to teach us to love. If you, who are perfect and glorious and all-powerful can be so humble, we want to be humble, too. Amen.

Week 41:
Freedom

What is your favorite sacrament, and why
(baptism, holy Eucharist, reconciliation, confirmation,
matrimony, holy orders, anointing of the sick)?

_____

*Now the Lord is the Spirit, and where the Spirit of the Lord
is, there is freedom. All of us, gazing with unveiled face on
the glory of the Lord, are being transformed into the same
image from glory to glory, as from the Lord who is the Spirit.*

2 Corinthians 3:17–18

Day 1: Holy souls in purgatory, we offer our work and prayers for you today. In return, please pray for us to be truly free from anything that comes between us and God. Real freedom is being our true selves, the way God made us. God wants us to be pure and holy, quick to forgive, hard-working, cheerful, and grateful for our blessings. Help us with your prayers so we can bring great love and hope to all we meet today. Holy souls in purgatory, pray for us. Amen.

Day 2: Dear guardian angels, human beings are made in the image and likeness of God, and when we trust in God, he keeps changing us for the better. This miracle is a great gift, and it happens in our souls. Help us to remember that when we are gentle and kind, we "look" like God. Today we ask for your prayers to help us to bring the beautiful, smiling face of God to all we meet. Guardian angels, pray for us. Amen.

Day 3: Dear St. Joseph, you took care of Jesus and Mary for many years, loving them with your whole heart. How radiant and beautiful your love must have been. Sometimes it's hard to love the people closest to us, so we need to grow in patience and understanding. From now on, whenever someone upsets me at home, help me to offer that suffering as a sacrifice to God. Like Jesus on the cross, we are called to help save souls through the offering of our own pain and sorrow. Thank you, St. Joseph, for your example of patience. Amen.

Day 4: Jesus, in the holy Eucharist, your Real Presence at Mass is absolutely amazing. What appears to be a simple host made of bread becomes your precious Body, Blood, Soul, and Divinity. As we eat your Body and Blood, we welcome you into our bodies and our souls. Thank you for nourishing us and filling us with the holy light of your love. Lord Jesus, present in the Blessed Sacrament, have mercy on us. Amen.

Day 5: Jesus, when I am tired or sad, I want to curl up into your Sacred Heart. Your tender and loving heart always has room for me. Whenever I come to you in prayer, you welcome me and wrap me up in your love. Help me to grow strong in faith and virtue so that as I grow up I will become a sanctuary of love for others. Sacred Heart of Jesus, have mercy on us. Amen.

Week 42:
The Ascension

*Has there ever been a time when you were sad
and then someone came to comfort you?*

---

*When they had gathered together they asked him, "Lord, are
you at this time going to restore the kingdom to Israel?" He
answered them, "It is not for you to know the times or seasons that the Father has established by his own authority.
But you will receive power when the holy Spirit comes upon
you, and you will be my witnesses in Jerusalem, throughout
Judea and Samaria, and to the ends of the earth." When he
had said this, as they were looking on, he was lifted up, and
a cloud took him from their sight. While they were looking in-
tently at the sky as he was going, suddenly two men dressed
in white garments stood beside them. They said, "Men of Galilee, why are you standing there looking at the sky? This Jesus
who has been taken up from you into heaven will return in
the same way as you have seen him going into heaven."*

Acts 1:6–11

Day 1: Come Holy Spirit, open our minds and hearts to all that
God wants to teach us today and all through the school week.
You are the third person of the Blessed Trinity, and we adore
you and praise you for your glorious power and your tender love
for us. You have come to earth to inspire us and help us to be
holy. You guide Holy Mother Church and bring your healing
power to us through the sacraments of baptism, Eucharist, and
reconciliation. Thank you, Holy Spirit, for dwelling within us.
We love you. Amen.

Day 2: Glorious angels, you appeared to the apostles as they watched Jesus go up into heaven. They must have been amazed and shocked at the way he rose right up to into the sky while they were held firmly to the earth by gravity. How thrilling to see the power of God in action. And yet, Jesus' dear friends must have been sad to see him leave that day. Thank you, dear angels of God, for the comfort and kindness you brought to the friends of Jesus. Help us to be his friends, too, by trusting that Jesus lives forever in our hearts. Amen.

Day 3: Glorious St. Joseph, on the day that Jesus rose into heaven, did you run to greet him? Were you waiting by the gates of heaven with your arms open? How wonderful it must have been to see each other again. In heaven there is no suffering, no loneliness, no sadness, no separation. Saint Joseph, pray for us, that we may enjoy the bliss of heaven with all those we love. Amen.

Day 4: Dear Jesus, even though you ascended into heaven, body and soul, we know that you come to us at every Mass, in the Blessed Sacrament. When we see the host lifted up at the altar, help us remember your sacrifice on the cross and thank you for loving us. When we welcome you into our hearts, we become living tabernacles because we carry you to the world everywhere we go. Lord Jesus, Son of God, we adore you and we praise you. Amen.

Day 5: Sacred Heart of Jesus, you are so generous. You have given us every good gift, especially the gift of yourself on the cross. After your ascension, you sent the Holy Spirit to be with us always, leading and encouraging us to grow in holiness. We are members of the royal family of heaven through our baptism, and the gifts of the Holy Spirit help us to be our truest, happiest selves. Bless us with grateful hearts so that your light will shine in our lives now and forever. Amen.

SECTION NINE

Led by the Spirit

Week 43:
Pentecost

What are your hopes for the future of the Church and the world?

_____

When the time for Pentecost was fulfilled, they were all in one place together. And suddenly there came from the sky a noise like a strong driving wind, and it filled the entire house in which they were. Then there appeared to them tongues as of fire, which parted and came to rest on each one of them. And they were all filled with the holy Spirit and began to speak in different tongues, as the Spirit enabled them to proclaim...Then Peter stood up with the Eleven, raised his voice, and proclaimed to them...'"It will come to pass in the last days,' God says, 'that I will pour out a portion of my spirit upon all flesh. Your sons and your daughters shall prophesy, your young men shall see visions, your old men shall dream dreams...And I will work wonders in the heavens above and signs on the earth below.'"

Acts 2:1–4, 14, 17, 19

Day 1: Come, Holy Spirit, burning fire of God's love. Anoint us and bless us as we start a new week of learning and growing closer to God. When you anointed the apostles, they were no longer afraid of any danger and were able to talk with people from all over the world. We trust that this same holy power is great enough to help us understand our school lessons and the teachings of the Church. Your power is great enough to help us understand our own hearts and the needs of the people around us. We praise you, Holy Spirit. You are our friend and guide. Amen.

Day 2: Lord God, thank you for our glorious guardian angels, who have watched over us since our birth and who love us. No matter what language we speak, our guardians understand our prayers and the desires of our heart. Our angels walk with us and love to pray for us. We are blessed by these heavenly friends throughout our lives, and we will meet our angels face-to-face in heaven. Holy guardian angels, pray for us. Amen.

Day 3: St. Joseph, you received amazing prophecies in your dreams so that God's holy plan could unfold. Your humble heart was open to the voice of God, and angels appeared to comfort and guide you as you labored to protect Jesus and Mary. Please ask God to give us a healthy humility, too, so that our hearts will be open to God's voice every day. Remind us that we are very precious to our good, all-powerful God. We can depend on him and trust in his love for us. Holy St. Joseph, pray for us. Amen.

Day 4: Dear Jesus, we adore you in the Blessed Sacrament. Each time we receive you, help us think only of you so that your presence fills our souls. If our thoughts are distracted, send your Holy Spirit into our minds and hearts to show us the precious gift and awesome power of your love for us. You have the power to change our lives and the lives of all those we love. Remind us to place all our hopes and worries in your loving care, at every Mass. Jesus, have mercy on us. Amen.

Day 5: Blessed Mary, most pure, through the power of the Holy Spirit, you became the Mother of God. Help us always be ready to open our hearts to God's will for our lives so the Holy Spirit can use us to bring Jesus into the world. You are our beautiful mother, given to us by Jesus on the cross. You loved St. John and all of the other apostles with the tenderness of a mother, and you love us just as much. Oh, pure and holy Mother of God, pray for us now and at the hour of our death. Amen.

Week 44:
Transformation

Did you know that Jesus can take our ordinary lives and make them extraordinary?

On the third day there was a wedding in Cana in Galilee, and the mother of Jesus was there. Jesus and his disciples were also invited to the wedding. When the wine ran short, the mother of Jesus said to him, "They have no wine." [And] Jesus said to her, "Woman, how does your concern affect me? My hour has not yet come." His mother said to the servers, "Do whatever he tells you." Now there were six stone water jars there for Jewish ceremonial washings, each holding twenty to thirty gallons. Jesus told them, "Fill the jars with water." So they filled them to the brim. Then he told them, "Draw some out now and take it to the headwaiter." So they took it. And when the headwaiter tasted the water that had become wine, without knowing where it came from (although the servers who had drawn the water knew), the headwaiter called the bridegroom and said to him, "Everyone serves good wine first, and then when people have drunk freely, an inferior one; but you have kept the good wine until now." Jesus did this as the beginning of his signs in Cana in Galilee and so revealed his glory, and his disciples began to believe in him.

John 2:1–11

Day 1: Dear holy souls in purgatory, through the burning fire of God's sweet love, you are being transformed and cleansed. Just as Jesus turned ordinary water into a fine wine, he is changing you and preparing you for heaven. What joy you must feel, even as you suffer, because you are moving closer and closer to Jesus. We offer our work, rest, and play for you today and ask God to bring you to heaven this very day. Holy souls in purgatory, pray for us so we may live lives worthy of our heavenly reward. Amen.

Day 2: Radiant Mother of God, at the wedding feast at Cana, Jesus called you "woman" because you asked him to perform a miracle out of mercy for a young couple. It would be the very first miracle Jesus ever performed in public. He honored you with a very great title because the Bible says that "the woman" will crush the head of Satan by bringing God's mercy to the whole world (Genesis 3:15). We know that you are Queen of Heaven and that, in your great love for us, you say, "Do whatever Jesus tells you." Amen.

Day 3: Lord, we thank you for our families. Our parents, grandparents, and others who love us and care for us are so precious. They are holy gifts from you, Lord. Help us to appreciate them and to pray for them every day. We are all sinners, and we all fail sometimes, but you never stop loving us. Help us to be merciful, like you, and to be thankful for our families. Inspire us to listen, to be helpful, and to treat each other with respect. We know this is pleasing to you, dear loving Lord Jesus. Amen.

Day 4: Dear Jesus, sometimes you tell me to do something and I don't want to do it. Maybe I'm having trouble forgiving someone who hurt me, or I don't feel like doing my chores or obeying my parents. I know you understand my struggles and that you are very patient with me. I ask you today, in this very moment, to give me a deep desire to please you in all that I say and do. When I sometimes fail, remind me how much you love me, in spite of my sins. Jesus, my Lord and my God, have mercy on me. Amen.

Day 5: Jesus, you revealed your glory to the people at the wedding feast by performing an act of kindness. The wine was running out, and the bride and groom were embarrassed. But you came to their rescue and turned ordinary water into a delicious wine. Jesus, we praise you for the ways you make our celebrations more joyful. Help us remember that any time we drink a glass of water or light a candle in our homes or at church, you are with us, bringing us refreshment, light, and joy. We love you, Jesus. Amen.

Week 45:
The Eucharist

The Israelites ate manna, little flakes of bread that appeared, miraculously, on the ground each day.
Now Jesus feeds us his own Precious Body and Blood from the altar, at Mass. What would you like to say to Jesus?

———————————————

I am the bread of life. Your ancestors ate the manna in the desert, but they died; this is the bread that comes down from heaven so that one may eat it and not die. I am the living bread that came down from heaven; whoever eats this bread will live forever, and the bread that I will give is my flesh for the life of the world.

John 6:48–51

Day 1: Dear God, when your Chosen People were hungry in the desert, you fed them miraculous bread. Now that you have given us the Eucharist, we have miracle bread, too. But when we receive holy Communion, it isn't just bread that we receive; we receive your precious Body and your precious Blood. You are the Living Bread who has come down from heaven to give us eternal life. You are all holy, all good, and all powerful. Merciful Jesus, we love you. Amen.

Day 2: Dear guardian angel, each time I go to Mass, please ask God to give me a thankful heart and help me to see the reminders of his presence all around me: the priest, the Bible readings, the tabernacle, the sanctuary light, the people, the artwork, and the music that helps us lift our hearts to God. Most of all, help me to treasure the presence of Jesus in the holy Eucharist. Thank you, holy angel, for your constant prayers for my soul. Amen.

Day 3: Lord Jesus, you gave everything to save us: your body, your blood, your soul and divinity. Strengthen us to give everything we have out of love for you. Take our past, our present, and our future and make of it what you will. Heal our wounds and fill us with hope. Increase our faith and make our hearts generous and courageous, like yours. Loving Lord, the more we give, the more we receive. Help us give all that we have out of love for you. Amen.

Day 4: Jesus, Bread of Life, we believe in you, we adore you, and we ask for your holy mercy for all the souls in purgatory. We are all one family and one body in you, Lord Jesus. Our family connection doesn't end when someone dies. Our loved ones continue to need our prayers and our offerings. Each time we attend Mass, inspire us to offer your precious Body and Blood for these holy souls. Jesus, have mercy on us. Amen.

Day 5: Sacred Heart of Jesus, you did not come to earth to be rich or to be in power over others. You came as a humble child. Then you spent your life serving and loving others. You fed people, you healed them, and you taught them to love. Help us to love our teachers and parents because they work very hard to feed us with knowledge, to bring us to the healing power of the sacraments, and to teach us the importance of loving as you love. Almighty and gentle Lord, have mercy on us. Amen.

Week 46:
Gifts of the Spirit

What gift of the spirit would you like to have?

_____

There are different kinds of spiritual gifts but the same Spirit; there are different forms of service but the same Lord; there are different workings but the same God who produces all of them in everyone. To each individual the manifestation of the Spirit is given for some benefit. To one is given through the Spirit the expression of wisdom; to another the expression of knowledge according to the same Spirit; to another faith by the same Spirit; to another gifts of healing by the one Spirit; to another mighty deeds; to another prophecy; to another discernment of spirits; to another varieties of tongues; to another interpretation of tongues. But one and the same Spirit produces all of these, distributing them individually to each person as he wishes.

1 Corinthians 12:4–11

Day 1: Holy Spirit of God, from you we receive everything good and holy: wisdom, knowledge, faith, healing, and so much more. You have made each of us for a purpose, and you have a plan to use our gifts and talents to help save the world. Lord, living in your love is a great adventure. Today we ask that you show each of us a way to serve you by serving others. Inspire us to be kind, forgiving, and fair with each other. Show us how you are calling us to love. Amen.

Day 2: My God, thank you for giving me a very special angel to pray for me, day and night, throughout my whole life. Through the intercession of my guardian angel, grant that I may learn to use all my gifts in ways that please you. You are incredibly good and generous, and I want to show how thankful I am by living my life totally for you. Dear Lord, make my heart pure and gentle so that your powerful light can shine through me and out to the world. Amen.

Day 3: God, inspired by your Holy Spirit, many prophecies in the Old Testament Scriptures proclaimed the exciting truth that you sent your beloved Son into the world to save us from our sins. Jesus is the only person in all of history whose birth was foretold. Lord, send us your Spirit. Speak to our hearts and help us to proclaim hope and salvation to all the world. Amen.

Day 4: Lord, you have made each human being unique and precious in your sight. Fill us with awe when we think of this truth. Every boy and girl from every country and every race is beautiful in your eyes. Help us to see each other the way you do, and fill our hearts full of wisdom and love. Show us the best in ourselves and teach us to look for the best in each other. Lord, have mercy. Amen.

Day 5: Holy Spirit of God, you are the source of all miracles, and you fill us with the very life of the Blessed Trinity. Through your power, each of us is given special gifts that help heal our broken world. Teach us to be reverent in our prayers, so that, in the quiet of our hearts, you will be able to speak to us and lead us to the holy paths you have made for our lives. No matter what anyone else thinks of us, your light shines within us. Amen.

Week 47:
Fruits of the Spirit

Which fruit of the spirit do you find in yourself?
How about someone you know?

_____

In contrast, the fruit of the Spirit is love, joy, peace, patience, kindness, generosity, faithfulness, gentleness, self-control. Against such there is no law.

Galatians 5:22–23

Day 1: Most Holy Trinity, you are one God and yet you are three persons: Father, Son, and Holy Spirit. When we pray the Our Father—the perfect prayer—we speak the words of Jesus to our beloved Father and we are touched by the Holy Spirit. Bring us the fruits of the Spirit each day so that we will live our lives in joy, in peace, and in great love. As you inspire us to be generous, faithful, and gentle, we will grow in the self-control that makes our lives truly virtuous and victorious. Amen.

Day 2: Dear Holy Spirit, we thank you and we praise you for the mysterious and beautiful ways you give us more and more life every day. Help us to pray with joy, humility, and the peace that only you can give so that we will no longer be worried about anything. With your help, we will live with more courage and confidence. You never take your eyes off us for a moment, and your love never leaves us. Especially in times of suffering, Lord, you watch over us with great affection. Amen.

Day 3: Spirit of God, your ways are perfect. No laws can stand in the way of your love. No walls can keep love out, and no darkness can prevent your light from shining. No matter where we go or what we do, your powerful love is right there, holding us in existence. We are here on earth because you will it. Help us to be brave and stand up for our faith so that the light and power of your love for us will spread throughout the world. Amen.

Day 4: Lord, you are gentle with us, even though your power is infinite and awesome. You are generous with us, even though we can give you nothing in return but our weak, human love. You are faithful to all of your promises to help us in all our needs, even though we often forget about you. Make us like you, spreading joy and peace wherever we go. Amen.

Day 5: Come, Holy Spirit, refresh our souls when we are tired and discouraged. This world will one day pass away, and all of your children will live together in heaven forever. Brighten our hearts, and send us human friendships that bring out the best in us. Give us companions full of your peace, joy, and kindness so that we can learn from them and grow in holiness. Inspire us to smile at those who are lonely and to speak words of friendship and encouragement. We can bring refreshment to those who are weary. Amen.

Week 48:
Confidence

*Instead of worrying, name some situations
where you can show you are confident in God's love.*

We know that all things work for good for those who love God, who are called according to his purpose. For those he foreknew he also predestined to be conformed to the image of his Son, so that he might be the firstborn among many brothers...What then shall we say to this? If God is for us, who can be against us? He who did not spare his own Son but handed him over for us all, how will he not also give us everything else along with him?

Romans 8:28–29, 31–32

Day 1: Dear holy souls in purgatory, your victory will come! God promises to make great good come from every life offered to him. Even though you regret the times you failed to love others, God is washing your soul clean and bringing hope to those you left behind. May our prayers and works help lift you up and bring you joy. Please remember to pray for us so our souls will be ready for heaven at all times. Amen.

Day 2: Jesus, you are our brother and Lord. It's wonderful to think about how you came to earth as a little baby, cradled in the arms of Mary and Joseph. When you became human, you made the rest of the human race holy. Help us remember that we are members of your royal family. Strengthen us with the Eucharist to behave and speak like true sisters and brothers of the most high king. Jesus, we love you. Have mercy on us. Amen.

Day 3: Dear guardian angels, sometimes we are afraid. It might be fear of another person or fear of failing at school or in sports. Sometimes, alone in the dark, we wonder if we are safe in our beds. But the Bible says, "If God is for us, who can be against us?" Pray for us every day, dear angels, that we will grow in faith, live with more peace, and have confidence in the love of God. Truly, with your help, we can become courageous saints. Amen.

Day 4: Loving Father, you gave your only Son, Jesus, to save our souls. It's hard for us to imagine what that must have been like. You are an infinitely loving Father, and you don't enjoy it when anyone suffers, including your Son, who died on the cross out of love for us. Help us to remember, Lord, that there is no greater gift than to lay down our lives for each other. We ask you to bless all those who risk their lives in noble service, including police officers, firefighters, and soldiers. God bless such brave men and women. Amen.

Day 5: Jesus, you said that if we asked for anything in your name, we would receive it. Help us to understand that we should always ask for holiness, above all. The spiritual gifts you want to give us are amazing and have the power to transform our lives. All together, we ask for every gift and blessing that you hold in your heart, waiting to pour them out for us. Give us every grace that we and our loved ones need, whether we know it or not. Jesus, we trust in you. Amen.

Week 49:
Gospel Values

Name something you don't enjoy doing that makes your home or school a better place. Then say why it's important to do it anyway.

———————————————

I urge you therefore, brothers, by the mercies of God, to offer your bodies as a living sacrifice, holy and pleasing to God, your spiritual worship. Do not conform yourselves to this age but be transformed by the renewal of your mind, that you may discern what is the will of God, what is good and pleasing and perfect.

Romans 12:1–2

Day 1: Lord, you are perfect, the model of all that we hope to become. You are the way to heaven, and people are happiest when they try to live by your laws. People in movies and on television sometimes dress or act in ways that are unhealthy and even sinful, yet they seem so happy and successful. Give us eyes to see what is real and what is false so we can live in freedom and peace instead of falling into temptation. Send us your spirit, Lord. Make us wise. Amen.

Day 2: Holy angels, you guard us and pray for us each day. You never stop adoring and praising God. Help us to be like you, always grateful for the goodness and beauty of God. Never cease to guide us into the paths of holiness that lead to our most joyful life here on earth and the perfect happiness of our true home in heaven. Thank you, holy angels. We look forward to seeing you in the presence of God, some glorious day. Amen.

Day 3: St. Joseph, you lived a life of great holiness and trust. You were willing to do whatever God asked of you, even when it was extremely hard. Pray for us so we will be able to hear the voice of God in our lives, as you did. Ask God to strengthen us and renew us in every way—minds, hearts, and bodies—so that we will be ready and willing to serve. Pray for our vocations, great St. Joseph. Amen.

Day 4: Dear Jesus, when we go to Mass, we see the priest hold up the host and the chalice and say the words of consecration. Then we see the crowds of people come, like little children, to be fed the Eucharist, our heavenly meal. Help us to see how humble and gentle you are, giving yourself completely to us at every Mass. Give us clear sight so we can see what is good and how we can be pleasing to you. We love you so much, dear Jesus. Help us to be more like you every day. Amen.

Day 5: Dear Jesus, in your heart we find safety and hope. You invite us to give you all of our fears and sadness. You offer us the joy of being loved completely and forever. No matter how bad we might feel about ourselves or about anything, you call us to come closer to you because you love us so much. Help us, Lord, to believe that you love us and help us to love you in return. The best gift we can give you is being kind to others, especially when the people in our lives disappoint us. Lord Jesus, fill us with your love. Amen.

Week 50:
Final Blessing

Remember your favorite lessons from this year and give thanks to God for every blessing.

Holy Father, keep them in your name that you have given me, so that they may be one just as we are....Consecrate them in the truth. Your word is truth. As you sent me into the world, so I sent them into the world. And I consecrate myself for them, so that they also may be consecrated in truth.

John 17:11, 17–19

Day 1: Sweet Holy Spirit, you are kind and merciful. We know you have a plan to bless every moment of our lives. Inspire us to take all of the lessons of the school year, hold them gratefully in our hearts, and then offer them back to you. Lead us into our break time confident that you will bring good out of our failures, as well as our accomplishments. There is nothing that cannot bear beautiful fruit through your holy power. Come, Holy Spirit. Amen.

Day 2: Father in heaven, all that is good, true, and beautiful comes from you. When you sent your only begotten Son, Jesus, into the world, it was because of your great love for us. Jesus is our Savior and Lord, the greatest gift the human race has ever received. Jesus showed us how to be our best selves by serving others in generosity and humility. He showed us that our own suffering can help to save souls, too. Our Father, who art in heaven, we praise your holy name. Amen.

Day 3: Lord, because of your goodness, every moment of our lives has purpose and meaning. In your kindness, you call us to love others through our ordinary work, play, and rest. Open our eyes to ways we can share your grace and mercy. Give us wisdom and increase our willingness to put the needs of others first. Show us how to be kinder, more patient, and more generous, all to your greater glory. Amen.

Day 4: Lord Jesus, we call our eucharistic celebration the holy Mass, which comes from a word that means "mission." After Mass, we are sent out to spread your holy word and your unconditional love to all we meet. Help us remember that we are agents of God on a mission from heaven. We ask all this in your holy name, Jesus Christ our Lord. Amen.

Day 5: Immaculate Heart of Mary, wrap us all in your protective mantle and keep us close to you, all the days of our lives. As school time ends, a new phase begins, and we are joyful to think of summer days and time outdoors. Help us to remember, each time we gaze up into a blue sky, that your blue mantle is stretched over the world and your immaculate heart is full of love for us. When the sky is cloudy, remind us that we are tucked into the quiet shelter of your beautiful heart. Mary, conceived without sin, pray for us, our families, our teachers, and all who have strengthened us throughout the school year. Amen.

PRAYERS FOR
SPECIAL
OCCASIONS

A Moment of Silence *(invite God into your heart for one full minute, as you gaze upon a beautiful religious image: crucifix, icon, statue, holy card, etc.)*

Dear God, we know that you speak to us through all that is beautiful. As we look upon this image, we ask you to touch our hearts and speak to our souls as only you can. As we meditate in silence, send us your holy peace. Teach us, Lord, to hear your gentle voice that guides us day by day. Amen.

Advent (at the start)

Jesus, it is with great excitement that Advent begins, and we prepare to celebrate your holy birth. Help us remember that Advent is also a time of getting ready, a time to reflect and try to become better. Give us the grace to honor your birthday with hearts full of enthusiasm for serving others. Show us how we can be helpful at home, at school, and anywhere we visit during this holy season. We want to wish you the happiest birthday ever. Amen.

Annunciation

Holy angel Gabriel, you were sent by God to the Blessed Virgin Mary, when she was a young teenager. To this pure and innocent girl, you announced God's holy plan to make her the most blessed mother who ever lived: the mother of Jesus. Help us trust that God has a holy plan for our lives, too, and pray that—like Jesus—we will love the Blessed Mother with all our hearts. Amen.

Ash Wednesday

God, it is amazing that out of ordinary dust you formed the first human being. Through our baptism, human beings become adopted members of your royal family. Knowing you love us so much makes us glad to repent of our sins, out of love for you. Give us the strength to grow in virtue and to honor the holy sacrifice of Jesus on Calvary. Amen.

Asking for Prayer Intentions

Knowing that we are loved by God and that he hears all of our prayers, we ask for everything we need for ourselves and others, both here and around the world...
[Say intentions]
[Say] Dear Jesus, we trust in you.
Amen.

Before an Exam

Loving Lord, we have done our best to prepare, and now it is time to test our knowledge. Thank you for our angelic companions, who help us to become the best people we can be one day at a time. Through their prayers, grant us clear minds and your holy peace, Lord Jesus. Amen.

Birthday Blessing

On this special day, Lord God, *[name]* was born. You have a special plan and purpose for his/her life, and he/she is a blessing to all of us. We thank you and praise you, Lord, for the gift of *[name]*. Help us appreciate him/her and to learn from his/her gifts and good actions. May he/she and all those he/she loves be greatly blessed on this special day, in the name of the Father, and of the Son, and of the Holy Spirit. Amen.

Bless Our Studies and Our Chores

Lord, you sanctify us through the work we do, whether at home, at school, or anywhere else. Thank you for teaching us to give of ourselves in so many new ways. Whatever good we do, we offer to you now and always. Bless all our efforts and help us to bless others by performing every task with loving care and good cheer. Amen.

Blessing of Animals

Dear St. Francis, all of nature shows us the beauty of God. Watch over these creatures, who were made by God to bring joy into our lives. They are so innocent. They remind us to be innocent, too. We place them in your loving care, in the name of the Father, and of the Son, and of the Holy Spirit. Saint Francis, intercede for us. Amen.

Blessing of the Books

Thank you, Lord, for a new school year. These books are a precious gift from you, and we are happy to receive them. Help us to use them well and to treat them with respect, since through them you will strengthen us and lead us closer to discovering our true vocations. Guide us and mold us into our best selves so we can give glory to you with our lives. Amen.

Classroom Blessing

Lord, fill this space with your holy love and mercy. Help us to see you in every person who shares this space with us, to see the best in ourselves, and the best in each other. Teach us to be gentle, open to learning and hard work, and grateful for the gift of our teachers. We ask this in your holy name, Lord Jesus. Amen.

End of School Day

Lord, we thank you for another day together.
Bless our teachers and send your angels to guide us
safely home. When we arrive, grant us the grace to
think of others, not ourselves, and to be of help to
everyone in our family. Jesus, we love you. Amen.

End of Homeschooling Day

Lord, we thank you for another beautiful day with you.
Bless our parents and all who have enriched our lives.
Fill our home with your holy peace and help us to be
grateful for every lesson and every struggle that draws
us closer to you. Jesus, we trust in you. Amen.

End of Religious-Education Class:

Lord, we thank you for another lesson about your love.
Bless our teacher, our pastor, our families, and all who
share their Catholic faith with us. Fill our parish with
a spirit of hope, humility, and trust, and help everyone
to find their true mission in God. Jesus, we adore you.
Amen.

Exaltation of the Holy Cross (September 14)

Holy St. Helen, it was through your prayerful search
that the true cross was discovered and preserved
for the Church. We tenderly venerate the holy cross
of Jesus Christ upon which he was crucified so long
ago. For our sins he suffered and died, innocent and
unwavering. He never complained of the injustice nor
condemned those who harmed him. Pray for us, St.
Helen, that we will always be willing to take up our
own crosses without complaint. Amen.

Farewell to a Student

Lord, it is with sadness that we say goodbye to our friend, [name]. Thank you for the gift of his/her friendship. Bless him/her in the new adventure that awaits him/her, and send him/her onward with every grace and blessing. Take care of all his/her needs and smooth the path ahead so that he/she will find much joy, friendship, and peace in his/her new surroundings and a profound sense of your presence in his/her life now and forever. We ask this in your holy name, Lord Jesus. Amen.

Farewell to a Teacher

Lord, it is hard to say goodbye to [name], but we are grateful for all the time we have spent together. Bless our dear teacher, [name], for all the patience, kindness, creativity, and love that he/she has shared with us. She/he has worked unselfishly to educate us, and we know this is a rare gift. Help us to always treasure the blessing of our time together and never forget to be thankful. Amen.

Fresh Ideas

Come, Holy Spirit. From you, we know that an infinite wellspring of creativity is available to pour forth and bless both our education and our recreation. Be with us and inspire us with new possibilities and fresh approaches to the tasks at hand. All glory and honor to you, our Lord. Amen.

Fresh Start (two options)

Precious Lord, sometimes we feel we are doomed to fail at what seemed, at first, to be a great undertaking. Be with us and refresh us, Lord. Reawaken us to the possibilities hidden in our frustrations. You make all things new, by grace, and we trust in you to provide. Amen.

Precious Lord, today got out of hand. We just couldn't seem to work together, regardless of the reason why. Help us accept the days when little is accomplished and remember that it's not great deeds that please you but a contrite heart and a gentle spirit. Help us accept each other in a spirit of forgiveness, knowing that, when we show mercy, we make you smile. Amen.

Immaculate Conception (December 8)

Dearest Mother Mary, immaculate from the moment of your conception, you are our most pure, most holy queen. Since you watch over us with great tenderness and protect us with your prayers, help us honor you with good and reverent behavior at church, at home, and at school. Mary, mother of Jesus and our mother, pray for us, that we may be made holy. Amen.

Lent

Jesus, Lent is such a grace-filled time. It is the perfect time to go a little deeper into our friendship with you. Help us, Lord, to heed your call to come closer. Show us what needs to change in our habits and attitudes, for us to become more like you. Give us the grace to repent of our sins and to forgive others, since you are merciful and kind. Help us to get real and get humble. We love you, Jesus. Amen.

Memorial Day

Saint Sebastian, patron of soldiers and martyr to the Christian faith, we ask you to watch over all military personnel. We invoke your protection especially for our friends, family, and neighbors who are in harm's way at home or abroad. Keep them safe in spirit, mind, and body, and through their trials and sufferings bring them ever closer to the Sacred Heart of Jesus. Intercede without ceasing for the souls of all the men and women who have given their lives or their health in the service of their country. Saint Sebastian, pray for us. Amen.

Our Lady of Guadalupe (December 12)

Holy Virgin of Tepeyac, beloved Patroness of the Americas, you appeared to the humble St. Juan Diego on a hillside in Mexico and imprinted your likeness on the cloth of his tilma. Millions of pilgrims have come to pray at the site and to venerate the miraculous image that defeated paganism and brought Christianity to the Mexican people. Help us, beautiful Mother of Guadalupe, to have faith in your Son, Jesus Christ, and to remember your powerful love for all of your children. Amen.

Our Lady of the Rosary (October 7)

Lady of the Holy Rosary, your prayers for us are tender and sweet, but also powerful. When we call upon you for help in distress, you unfailingly come to our aid. Beautiful Mother, we thank you for teaching us we can count on your help, as well as your example of virtue and trust. Thank you for your humility, your courage, and your confidence in God. Through the daily recitation of the Holy Rosary, inspire and equip us to give our own lives wholeheartedly to God; to trust the Holy Spirit to guide our lives; and to lovingly bear Christ to the world. Amen.

Our Mother of Perpetual Help (June 27)

Dearest Mother of Perpetual Help, thousands have been healed, inspired, and converted through your miraculous image. As we gaze at the Christ Child, we notice that his hands rest in yours, bestowing on you every gift of grace so that you are free to pour them into our hearts. You never fail to help us, especially when we call upon you with confidence and affection. Mother of Perpetual Help, we love you. Amen.

Our Lady's Mantle (protection)

Dearest Mother Mary, wrap us in your blue mantle and protect us from every danger, physical or spiritual. Cradle us against your immaculate heart and carry us to the throne of your divine Son, Jesus, where no evil can approach us and no threat disrupt our peace. Amen.

Prayer for a Sick Child

My divine physician, Jesus, *[name]* is in need of rest, comfort, and healing. Send your holy angels to her/his bedside to fill his/her heart with courage. Bless those who care for him/her, and provide for all their needs. We long to see *[name]* again radiant with health and vigor. Come to our aid, precious Lord. Amen.

Prayer for Our Nation

Mother Mary, under the title of the Immaculate Conception, we give you our hearts. Watch over our nation and guide us, dear Mother, that we may be a people of wisdom, virtue, and selfless devotion to God and neighbor. Bless our leaders, that they may discover in themselves a wellspring of Christian love and self-sacrifice. Bless our people so we may approach every obstacle to peace in a spirit of joy, courage, and confidence. Teach us, immaculate Virgin Mary, how to say "yes" to God, as you did, and through your prayers, bring his holy kingdom to this earth. Amen.

Prayer for Parents

Dear God, please bless our mothers and fathers. Give them the wisdom and strength they need to watch over us and guide us into lives of virtue. Grant them a spirit of humble leadership so we may be inspired to follow their example and walk in the footsteps of Christ. Comfort them when they are stressed, provide for them when they are in need, and inspire us to treat them with the respect and reverence they deserve. Amen.

Prayer for the Missions

Jesus, we are all members of your mystical body, and you have a task for each of us. Together we bring your love to the world in many different ways. Some of us are called to journey to foreign lands and serve in the mission fields, far from family and friends. Bless our missionaries—priests, religious, and laypeople—who have left comfort behind to follow you more closely. Give them the grace to love without limits, as you do. Let us never forget the beauty and nobility of their daily sacrifice. Amen.

St. Patrick's Day

Holy St. Patrick, you defeated the pagan druids in Ireland because of your great faith in the one true God. Pray for us so we may be faithful to our Lord, Jesus Christ, even when it may be unpopular to be a Christian. Inspire us to shine the light of truth to all we meet. Saint Patrick, pray for us. Amen.

Seeing Jesus in Every Face (respect)

Dear Jesus, I long to look into your eyes and see your holy face. Help me to remember that you live inside every human person. You have given each of us a special dignity. From now on, whenever I speak to another person, give me the grace to see that I am speaking to you, my brother and Lord. Any act of kindness, I do to you, but any act of cruelty or harm, I also do to you. Forgive me for any hurt I have caused, Lord Jesus, and help me to respect every human life at all times. From now on, Lord, no matter who I meet in the course of my day, it will be your face I see. Amen.

Time of Tragedy

Jesus, you are good and gentle. It is never your will to hurt us, and you are always close to us when we suffer. Because of your great power, you can take any sad thing and make great good come from it. When you died on the cross, your sacrifice opened the gates of heaven to us, for all eternity. We only have to accept your mercy and repent of our sins. Please bless everyone who is in pain and sorrow because of *[mention the loss]*, and bring us lasting peace of spirit, mind, and body. We ask this in your holy name, Lord Jesus. Amen.

Valentine's Day

Lord God, all love and light comes from you. Every friendship, every love story, every act of heroism is an expression of your sacred heart. Thank you for the example of good St. Valentine, who gave his life in the name of love. Saint Valentine, pray for us. Amen.

Welcome a New Student

Lord, it is an honor to walk this road of life together. Thank you for sending us a new brother/sister in Christ to share our journey. Bless this time of learning, growing, and becoming what you call each of us to be, and inspire us to encourage and welcome our new friend. We ask for your blessing on *[name]* and on everyone here, in the name of the Father, and of the Son, and of the Holy Spirit. Amen.

Welcome a New Teacher

Almighty God, you make all things new. Thank you for sending *[name]* to teach us and lead us in our time of need. Our new teacher is a wonderful blessing, and we promise to make him/her feel completely welcome. Help us to respect and honor him/her, as he/she helps us discover the very best in ourselves. We ask all this in your holy name, Lord Jesus. Amen.

GLOSSARY

- A -

abounds: Something that is found in abundance (large quantities).

absolution: The spiritual cleansing associated with God's forgiveness of our sins. We receive the words of absolution from a priest during the sacrament of reconciliation, but it is Christ who forgives our sins.

adore: To gaze upon someone or something with deep love and appreciation.

ancient: To the modern reader, *ancient* means "very old, dating before the end of the Roman Empire in the late fifth century." In Scripture, the word *ancient* refers to times already long past, before the time of the biblical writer.

anoint: To ritually bless and dedicate, usually with oils, in the name of God. Anointing in Catholicism is associated with sacramental rituals, such as baptism, confirmation, holy orders, and anointing of the sick. The anointing of the ancient biblical kings was a blessing intended to demonstrate the new king's willingness to serve the one true God. The apostles were anointed in service of the Church, with the Holy Spirit and tongues of fire, at Pentecost.

archangel: A powerful, high-ranking angel. The three archangels mentioned in the Bible are Michael, Gabriel, and Raphael. The existence of angels is a truth of the Catholic faith (see the *Catechism of the Catholic Church,* 328). Angels are pure spirits who can appear in human form, if they choose. They belong to Christ and exist to serve God and act as messengers to the human race (see *CCC* 329). They are extraordinarily intelligent, immortal beings, possessing free will.

authority: In the biblical sense, authority refers to the right to lead the people of God, to help resolve conflicts, and to pass judgments regarding infractions against God's laws. It may seem paradoxical to modern sensibilities, but the obedience blessing found in Deuteronomy 28 shows that God's authority is a gift shared with his people when we are humbly obedient to his laws.

awe: A fruit of the Holy Spirit in which the soul is in a state of amazement mingled with a profound and joyful humility. Awe is the soul's recognition of something greater than itself, a recognition that lifts us outside our ordinary way of seeing and provides a glimpse of the mysteries of God.

- B -

begotten: To beget is to procreate; so, when we refer to Jesus as God's only begotten Son, we express the fact that Jesus is not a created child of God, as we humans are, but proceeds directly from the Father's own divine nature. Jesus is the only begotten Son of God and is therefore one of three divine persons in the Holy Trinity.

beloved: Greatly loved, cherished, or treasured.

bestow: To give something freely.

Blessed Sacrament: Refers to the Body and Blood of Christ in the form of consecrated sacramental bread and wine at a celebration of the holy Eucharist; synonym for the Eucharist (see **Eucharist**).

blessing: Anything good that can be seen as coming from the goodness of God. For instance, the love of our families and friends, the ministry of the priesthood that brings us the sacraments, our physical or spiritual health, and so on. One can also refer to particular outcomes as blessings, especially when they occur in response to our prayers, such as when a person recovers from illness or it rains after a long draught. Blessings can also be prayerful words that call down graces from heaven, like saying grace before meals or praying over children at bedtime.

bountifully: Abundantly, graciously, or generously. For instance, God's graces flow bountifully when we place our trust in him.

burden: Something that is carried with difficulty. A heavy load of laundry could be considered a burden, for instance. But when we speak of faith, we associate burdens with worries and troubles that God uses to bless and strengthen us. One of many varied examples might be that a mother "burdened" with a sick child will see the beauty of her struggle to nurture her child as she grows in her capacity to love through sacrifice and dependence on God.

- C -

compulsion: An act, often of a repetitive nature, which cannot be controlled easily. We sometimes say that a person being coerced or compelled by another against his will is under compulsion.

confess: To speak aloud. For instance, we confess our sins to the priest in the sacrament of reconciliation. We also confess our love for God when we declare our faith to others.

confession: Refers to the sacrament of reconciliation, in which we confess our sins to a priest and receive forgiveness and grace from Jesus through the ritual words of absolution (see **absolution**).

console: To give comfort to another. Many believers experience the consoling love of God in prayer.

crucifixion: A brutal method of torture and execution used by first-century Romans in which the victim was stripped and tied or nailed to a wooden cross and left to die by asphyxiation, thirst, or exposure. Jesus was put to death by crucifixion but later rose from the dead.

- D -

debtors: Those who are in debt to others. When we borrow money, we become debtors. In the Scriptures, debts often refer to the spiritual debts owed due to our sins. Jesus Christ paid our spiritual debts by dying on the cross.

deeds: Actions or accomplishments. Very often the use of the word *deeds* refers to actions we take that speak well or ill of our personal character.

despair: A state of extreme hopelessness. In moments of despair, God's people are asked to make a courageous leap of faith and trust that God is intimately present to them, since our trust unleashes a powerful outpouring of healing and transforming graces.

diligent: When a person perseveres in the face of suffering. Diligence is an important virtue, which helps us put aside distractions and discouragements.

disability: A state that limits a person's movements, senses, or activities in some way. A disability can be intellectual, developmental, or physical.

distress: When we need help or are suffering in some way. It can refer to situations as well as feelings.

divine: Having to do with God, since God is infinite, eternal, all-knowing, and all-powerful. We can refer to Jesus as being divine because he is the second person of the Trinity and shares his nature with the Father and the Holy Spirit. We can also say that God's law, since it proceeds from him, is of divine origin.

dwell: To make a home in a particular place. The Bible speaks of God dwelling with his people, and Christians speak of God as dwelling in our souls. However, the word can also mean "to ponder over something," as when we dwell on the words of sacred Scripture and listen for the voice of the Holy Spirit.

- E -

endure: To sustain effort or maintain equilibrium under stress. It is not a griping, resistant attitude but an ability to embrace a struggle with tolerance and adapt to difficulty in a spirit of courage.

eternal: Something that has no beginning and no end but always exists. Christians refer to that which is eternal when speaking of God. God's nature is both eternal and infinite.

Eucharist: The Blessed Sacrament we receive in holy Communion. Catholics refer to the Mass as our "eucharistic feast." The word *Eucharist* comes from a Greek word that means "thanksgiving" (see **Blessed Sacrament**).

exalt: To praise or elevate someone in rank. When we exalt ourselves, Scripture promises, we will be humbled (see Luke 14). In other words, we should seek to exalt and glorify God, not ourselves.

exhort: To encourage someone to try harder. Exhortations often came from the Old Testament prophets, who were sent by God to admonish and motivate his people to love God more by faithfully following his laws.

exult: To rejoice. When the Scriptures describe trees and other aspects of nature as exulting, we understand it to mean that all of the created world joyfully expresses the beauty, power, and goodness of God. This quality of divine expression through creation refers to the "sacramentality" of nature.

- F -

fail: To fall short of a goal. For instance, if we have tried to be patient but have lost our temper, we can say that we failed to exemplify the virtue of patience. The beautiful part of failure is the opportunity it presents us to humble ourselves before God, trusting in his mercy. No matter how often we fall short, he is there within us, loving us with infinite compassion and urging us to try again.

fasting: To avoid consuming something we normally enjoy for the purpose of atoning for sin and practicing self-control. For instance, if we abstain from eating meat on Fridays or choose to consume only bread and water, we actively atone for our sins and those of the world. As a spiritual practice, those who fast often do so in solidarity with the hungry of the world and with the selfless and saving passion of Jesus Christ. Fasting can be a powerful element of a vibrant spiritual life and may take the form of abstaining from a favorite pastime (such as television or phone use), an occasion of sin (listening to gossip), or some form of sustenance (food and drink).

fortitude: A gift of the Holy Spirit and can be described as the courageous ability to persevere in spite of extreme hardship. The martyrs of the Church who willingly gave their lives rather than renounce their faith in Jesus are exemplars of this virtue. We ask the Holy Spirit to provide fortitude whenever we are tempted to give up hope.

foul: In the context of Ephesians 4, foul language refers to anything profane or crude. Christians are asked to choose their words with care so that we always lift others up and give glory to God. Since God speaks through all that is true, good, and beautiful, anything that is false, selfish, or morally repugnant is considered foul.

- G -

gift: The gifts of the Magi (or Wise Men) were freely given to Jesus as symbols of great honor: gold honored him as a royal person, frankincense honored his priesthood, while myrrh was a spice used to anoint the deceased, giving honor to his eventual sacrifice on the cross.

glorious: When we refer to God as glorious, we give honor to him by recognizing the truth of his radiant beauty and infinite power. God is glorious because he is good, holy, and magnificent beyond our capacity to fully grasp.

grace: God's favor (see *CCC* 1996) provided to help us respond to the Gospel. Without God's gracious help, we could not enter heaven, but because he loves us, he offers us his divine assistance. At baptism, we receive sacramental grace, which is a share in the very life of God. Sacramental grace prepares the soul to receive the more ordinary graces of our everyday lives.

grieve: To suffer following the agonizing loss of someone or something we love. Jesus showed us that it is not wrong to grieve when he cried at the tomb of his friend, Lazarus. Yet St. Paul reminds us in 1 Thessalonians 4 that we are to live joyfully in the expectation of being reunited in heaven, not fall into despair, the way people do who have no hope.

- H -

hallowed: Sacred. When we say in the Lord's prayer, "Hallowed be thy name," we remind ourselves that God's name is holy and deserving of reverence and respect.

heritage: Something important that is inherited, usually through families and nations. A person born to Italian parents can be said to have an "Italian heritage," for instance. The heritage of the ancient Jews was their faith in the one true God, as his Chosen People. As adopted children of God, our Catholic faith is our birthright, our identity, and our foundation of strength.

heroine: The feminine form of the word *hero*. A hero is someone known for noble or brave deeds (see **deeds**).

homage: A public act of deep respect. We are said to pay homage to God's great mercy when we kneel before a crucifix or genuflect before the Blessed Sacrament. We also pay homage to his goodness and faithfulness when we endeavor to imitate his holy ways. Acts of homage can bring us an intimate sense of the greatness of God.

hymns: Songs or poems that give glory to God. They may also honor the Blessed Mother, the angels, or the saints.

- I -

infinite: In the context of our faith, infinite refers to the limitlessness of God, who has always existed, always will exist, and has no limitations whatsoever. The idea of infinity in other contexts is generally a descriptor for anything that appears to be incalculably vast and immeasurable.

iniquities: Immoral acts. Simply put, they are sins.

inspire: To lift another outside of his or her ordinary disposition and give the person an expanded sense of what is possible. An inspired person is filled with a desire to act, often creatively, and feels empowered to accomplish the task ahead. When we speak of God's inspiration, we touch on the root meaning of the word *inspire*: to breathe in.

The Holy Spirit fills us with inspiration, like a breath of life-giving air, strengthening us to respond to God's call or bringing us insight into his holy mysteries.

intercession: The charitable act of praying on another's behalf, which all Christians are encouraged to practice. Christ is our one, true intercessor before the Father, but because of God's generosity, the baptized become members of the body of Christ. As members of his body, we are invited to participate in the salvation of the world through our good works and intercessory prayers. We are also urged to ask for intercessory prayers for our own needs, since we are a "communion of saints," a family held together by Christ. Praying for the dead is a powerful form of intercession. The souls in purgatory are intensely grateful when we pray for them.

- L -

lame: To be unable to walk normally due to illness or injury.

- M -

Magi: Members of a priestly class of people from ancient Persia. Their religion forbade sorcery, but they sought guidance through dreams and the study of the stars and planets—a kind of ancient astrology.

Mass: A time when the children of God gather to give thanks and praise to God, listen to the word of the Lord through sacred Scripture, and are nourished by Christ's Body and Blood in holy Communion.

mantle: A cloak. The Blessed Virgin Mary's mantle is often invoked when the faithful seek her maternal care. It is traditional to ask her to cover us in the mantle of her protection.

meek: To be gentle and humble, not proud or aggressive. In Matthew 5:5, Jesus says, "Blessed are the meek, for they will inherit the earth" (*New International Version* of the Bible).

mercy: A quality very like forgiveness, as when a guilty person is shown leniency by the very person who has the power to inflict punishment. In an act of mercy, the punishment is far less than is deserved or is taken away, altogether. When we are merciful, we image God, who is infinitely merciful, kind, and forgiving.

miraculous: An extraordinary occurrence that defies the laws of nature, as when Jesus healed the blind and the lame (see Matthew 15:30) or brought Lazarus back to life (see John 11). Miraculous events show the power of God and occur in many parts of the Bible, including the parting of the Red Sea (see Exodus 14:21), the miraculous catch of fish (see John 21:1–14), and the resurrection of Jesus Christ (see Luke 24).

mock: To make fun of in a cruel way. Jesus was mocked and beaten during his sacred passion.

mystery: Something we cannot know fully through reason alone. The term refers especially to any religious truth revealed to humanity through supernatural means. Some of the great mysteries of our faith include the dual nature of Jesus Christ (fully human and fully divine), his willingness to suffer for us in spite of his innocence, and the resurrection of Jesus from the dead.

- P -

petition: A solemn request. When we petition God in prayer, we are devoutly imploring his help with a specific concern. For example, we might offer petitions to God for our own sake or for the welfare of others. It is appropriate to ask God to provide for all our needs and to offer him loving praise and thanksgiving, confident that he hears our prayers and answers them according to his holy and perfect will.

pit (the): When sacred Scripture refers to "the pit," we understand the term to mean "hell." The image of a pit, in this case, describes a bottomless hole where there is no light, no love, and no hope—for all eternity. The damnation of a soul is never God's will. Hell is a spiritual state chosen by souls who refuse to repent and allow God's mercy to save them (see *CCC* 1037).

pledge: A solemn promise or agreement.

popular: In this instance it is understood to mean that a person is well regarded by his or her peers.

pride: Pride can be good or bad. When we take pride in doing our work well, we grow in the holy virtue of diligence. However, we can have a false sense of our own importance that makes us impatient with others, slow to forgive, or dishonest about our own failings. The remedy to sinful pride is to cultivate humility, ask God's forgiveness in the sacrament of reconciliation, and actively seek to repair any harm we have done.

prophet: Scripture tells us that prophets were men and women sent by God to communicate his will to his beloved people, especially during times of upheaval and disobedience. In his mercy, God enlightened the prophets through supernatural means to call his children to repentance and renewal. The prophets were often scholars of the ancient Jewish laws and preached and taught wherever God urged them to go, citing chapter and verse to the rebellious and offering them a fresh start.

prostrated: To lie flat on the ground, face down. To assume such a posture is a gesture of extreme humility and reverence.

purpose: In Scripture, we are often reminded that God has a purpose for our lives, which means that each of us has a special mission for which we were uniquely created. As members of the body of Christ, we each play a part in the salvation of the world when we faithfully and humbly seek to do God's will.

- R -

radiant: In Scripture, radiance is a quality of soul. When a person is described as "radiant," we may infer his or her holiness, a shining or glorious quality of loving service that is understood to be a reflection of the glory of God. Radiance is often used as a metaphor for the new life and supernatural freedom our souls experience through God's mercy.

remnant: A remaining part of something larger. In the life of the Christian, the word *remnant* refers to the faithful followers of Jesus who still remain on earth. Scripture tells us that the "faithful remnant" will persevere in keeping the Ten Commandments to the end and enjoy eternal life (see Romans 11:5 and Revelation 12:17).

repent: To be deeply sorry for having done something wrong, whether the act was a single instance or a lifetime of sinfulness. To sincerely repent, it is necessary to commit to avoiding the sin in the future and to make amends for the harm done to others. Repentance is the first step toward true freedom, a turning away from sin and toward God. When we repent, all of heaven rejoices (see Luke 15:10).

resound: To fill up a space with sound. In Scripture, rejoicing in the Lord is often described as a hymn resounding throughout all of creation (see Psalm 98:7 and Isaiah 42:12).

reverent: To behave with great respect and humility. We are reverent when we are quiet and prayerful during the consecration at Mass. We are reverent when we do the sign of the cross with care. Reverence for each other and for ourselves is appropriate, as well, since God dwells in each of our souls, and we should treat each other accordingly.

rituals: Acts that are repeated because they have meaning, as in the liturgical rituals of our faith. From ancient times, believers have been engaging in rituals that helped their communities stay in touch with their identity as children of God. For example, when we bless ourselves with holy water, we recall our baptism into the royal family of God and ask him to cleanse us of our sins, and when we genuflect before the tabernacle, we honor the Real Presence of Jesus, who comes humbly into our midst to save our souls.

- S -

sacred: Something that is set apart in a special way and dedicated to God. For example, we call the books of the Holy Bible "sacred Scripture" because they are the inspired and living word of God. Images are considered sacred if they depict persons or realities that are holy and worthy of veneration: for instance, the Sacred Heart, the Immaculate Heart of Mary, and the Divine Mercy. Relics of holy persons or objects can also be considered sacred, such as the physical remains of the saints or fragments of the true cross.

sacrifice: A selfless offering. We might offer our time, effort, or money to a worthy cause, or we might decide to fast and pray for the welfare of another person in need. In Christianity, willing acts of sacrifice continue to be a powerful way of drawing closer to Jesus Christ in union with his saving passion and death.

salvation: The joy of heaven for all eternity. By suffering and dying to pay the debt for our sins, Jesus offers us salvation in and through him. We cannot achieve the gift of salvation on our own but only through his free gift of grace. He does, however, require that we cooperate with that grace. He will not force salvation on us. We must accept it willingly by doing our best each day to follow in the footsteps of Christ and trust that he will do the rest.

sanctuary: A safe place (as in a wildlife refuge) but also a holy place. When we speak of the sanctuary in a Catholic church, we are referring to the altar and the area around it. The sanctuary usually (but not always) includes the tabernacle and the lectern. When we speak of the sanctuary of the heart, we are referring to the intimate center of the human person, where Jesus dwells.

scholars: Educated people who spend their lives studying, writing, and/or teaching in a particular topic area. In Catholicism, scholars might focus on sacred Scripture, Church history, or the documents of the Church.

secure: To be safe and unafraid. Many of the Psalms extol the peace and security found in God's faithful love and protection.

Sheol: An ancient Hebrew word for hell, a place for souls who refuse the mercy of God. The Greeks called this place of eternal torment and separation from God *hades*.

soul: The spiritual part of our humanity. Since the *Catechism* tells us that human beings are a meaningful unity of body and soul, uniting within our very nature the spiritual and physical worlds (see *CCC* 355), we should never think of the soul as simply residing in the body. After the Final Judgment, our souls will be reunited with our glorified bodies for all eternity.

- T -

tabernacle: A dwelling place, so we use this term to describe the special cabinet in a Catholic church where the consecrated host is stored. It is usually placed in a visible area so the congregation can feel free to adore the Real Presence of Christ within. There are special rules for the way a tabernacle must be constructed and kept secure, since it is very important that the Blessed Sacrament be protected from improper use. Often the tabernacle is an object of great beauty, to remind the faithful that it is our Lord who dwells within.

temple: A place of prayer and ritual sacrifice. The ancient Jews made pilgrimages to the temple in Jerusalem in honor of their most holy feast days in order to pray and make sacrificial offerings to God.

tomb: A place of burial, usually carved into the earth or made of stone. Caves have sometimes been used to entomb the dead.

trustworthy: The characteristic of someone who is known to be honest, reliable, and resistant to corruption.

- U -

universe: The cosmos, the seemingly limitless expanse of outer space, including every black hole, galaxy, and solar system. Science tells us that the universe is about thirteen billion years old and is expanding all the time, which supports the theory of a "primeval atom" (also known as the "big bang"). Like many scientific breakthroughs, this theory, put forth in the 1930s by Monsignor Georges Lemaitre, is an example of the Catholic Church's long tradition of supporting scientific inquiry.

- V -

vast: Immense, huge, gargantuan.

- W-

wisdom: The first and highest gift of the Holy Spirit. Wisdom helps us value the ways of God above the ways of the world to help us to be free of influences that are not holy. We should pray for wisdom every day.

wondrous: Something that has the power to enrapture and inspire us. For example, when we are moved by God's generosity, his goodness, or the beauty of creation, we might say that we have experienced God's wondrous love.

wretched: To be in a state of emotional or psychological poverty, as when a person falls into despair.

- Y -

yoke: A device for harnessing animals together, such as when oxen are fastened together under a crossbar to help them plow a field in unison. Christians will sometimes refer to being "yoked" to Christ, which means that they choose to serve him, taking him as their master, and seeking to follow in his footsteps. When Christ says, "My yoke is easy, and my burden light" (Matthew 11:30), he means that his ways are truth and life, not the wearying ways of the world.